THE MANY VOICES OF JOB

The Many Voices of

LOREN R. FISHER

CASCADE *Books* • Eugene, Oregon

THE MANY VOICES OF JOB

Copyright © 2009 by Loren R. Fisher. All rights reserved. Except for brief quotations in critical publications or reviews, no part of this book may be reproduced in any manner without prior written permission from the publisher. Write: Permissions, Wipf & Stock, 199 W. 8th Ave., Suite 3, Eugene, OR 97401.

Cascade Books
A Division of Wipf and Stock Publishers
199 W. 8th Ave., Suite 3
Eugene, OR 97401

www.wipfandstock.com

ISBN 13: 978-1-60608-656-8

Cataloging-in-Publication data:

Fisher, Loren R.

    The many voices of Job / Loren R. Fisher.

    xx + 112 p. ; 23 cm. Includes bibliographical references and indexes.

    ISBN 13: 978-1-60608-656-8

    1. Bible. O.T. Job—Criticism, interpretation etc. 2. Job (Biblical figure). 3. Bible. O.T. Job—Translating. I. Title.

BS1415.2 F5 2009

Manufactured in the U.S. A.

For Moïse

Our world is beautiful but hard.

We encounter beauty and pain.

He is able to see and stand;

Appreciation and courage

Reside within him constantly.

His accomplishments match his strength.

Yes, we are blessed by his presence.

Contents

Acknowledgments ix
Preface xi
Abbreviations xiii
Introduction xv

1 The Ancient Folktale of Job *1*
2 The Rebel Job *29*
3 Where Can Wisdom Be Found? *79*
4 The Speeches of Elihu *85*

Afterword 99
Bibliography 103
Index of Ancient Deities and Characters of Myth and Legend 107
Index of Ancient Documents 108
Index of Authors and Scholars 112

Acknowledgments

I want to thank the poet of Job 3–26 whose anger burned against the ancient story of Job, and whose fiery poem was extinguished by wrapping it in the ancient story of Job. This poet was buried, as were his words; his words were not set in stone. He cries out:

> O that my words would be written,
> Would be engraved on the stela,
> With an iron stylus and lead.
> They would be carved in rock as a witness."[1]

These lines express the wish of the poet, of his Job, and of a minority of great minds in the ancient Mediterranean world. The view of the rebel is important for our modern world. The questions, "Who hears the cries of the innocent?" "Why do the wicked live on?" and "Why me?" are still on the lips of many in our times.

I would like to express my thanks to a modern poet, namely, Archibald MacLeish, for his poetic drama, *J.B.* Also I want to thank Joseph Roth for his novel, *Hiob*. Many scholars have been helpful in writing this book, but three of them met most of my special needs. My friend Marvin H. Pope helped me at every turn. His Anchor Bible *Job* has been my mainstay. Edwin Good's translation, *In Turns of Tempest*, has been helpful, and Bruce Zuckerman's *Job The Silent* was extremely interesting for my work.

Some true friends have helped along the way: John B. Cobb Jr., Kevin Clark, Duane Smith, Stan Rummel, and K. C. Hanson, my editor at Cascade Books. I thank my wife, Jane Sheldon, for her careful reading and editing of this book and others before they go out the door.

The indexes were prepared by K. C. Hanson.

---

1. Job 19:23–24.

Preface

Many students of ancient Mediterranean literature could produce a good translation of Job, but no one is able give the public a perfect translation.[1] The book of Job is found in the Hebrew Bible, but even if you know Hebrew some of it is impossible to translate. The task is comparable to asking a good college student to read and translate *Beowulf*. I have been working on Job, off and on, for about fifty-five years, and I will probably work on it for the rest of my life.[2] What finally inspired me to publish this work in progress was a chance reading of Ralph Hone's book, *The Voice Out of the Whirlwind*,[3] in which he collected papers and materials about the book of Job for his students. Three essays caught my attention. All three of them deal with Archibald MacLeish and his play *J.B.*

The first two essays are by scholars from Union Theological Seminary in New York, Tom Driver and Samuel Terrien, the latter an expert on Job. Both reviewed MacLeish's play in *The Christian Century*, January 7, 1959.[4] In my opinion, they were too critical of a great play. In fact, Henry P. Van Dusen, who at that time was the president of Union Theological Seminary, seemed to agree with me, because in a later issue of *The Christian Century*[5] he was critical of both Driver and Terrien. Van Dusen wrote that their critiques were "one-sided, perverse and unconvincing." I believe Van Dusen had a good understanding of MacLeish. He also be-

---

1. The translations in this book were published in four of my earlier books. **The Ancient Folktale of Job** (Job 1–2, 27–31, 38–42) appeared in *Who Hears the Cries of the Innocent?* **The Rebel Job** (Job 3–26) was also in that volume. **The Rebel Job** can also be found in my books: *The Rebel Job*, *The Rebel Job: Revised Edition*, and *The Minority Report*, which also contains Job 28 and the speeches of Elihu. The translations are getting better, but perfection is beyond us.

2. N. H. Tur-Sinai wrote several books on Job during his active years, and some of them disagreed with the others.

3. Hone, *The Voice*, 282–97.

4. Driver, "Notable, Regrettable," 21–22; and Terrien, "*J.B.* and Job," 9–11.

5. Van Dusen, "Third Thoughts on *J. B.*," 106–7.

Preface

lieved that biblical scholars have helped to confuse the readers of Job. Van Dusen thought readers have a right to know that Job "is not *a* book but *two* books, or rather a magnificent poem encased in and encrusted by a prose introduction and conclusion which not only are obviously from a different hand and a different period and patently on an immeasurably lower spiritual as well as intellectual level, but which also contradicts in the most flagrant terms the very meaning and purpose and faith of the poem and go far to negate its message."[6] I would add that the poem and its author were framed in both meanings of that word. **The Ancient Folktale of Job** formed a frame that was ancient and ornate, and it ruined the inserted poem or dialogue. It caused both books to be misunderstood.

All of this has made it difficult for any modern treatment of Job, and it has also caused some confusion in MacLeish's work. However, it is amazing that even though the traditional ending of the folktale or **Job I**—where all is restored to him—is an earlier sub-theme in MacLeish's play, his real ending is from **Job II** or what I call **The Rebel Job** (chapters 3–26).[7]

Scholars have talked about these two books under one cover in Job for many years, but no one has really allowed them to stand alone as individual books. Instead most scholars have remained vague as to what is in each book. Many of my colleagues are willing to consider the poem **Where Can Wisdom Be Found?** and **The Speeches of Elihu** as later and separate additions;[8] but there is resistance to a two-book theory resulting in **Job I** and **Job II**. Many scholars seem to accept that there are two books in the book of Judges or even three books in Isaiah; but the tendency is to look at Job as a unity or only in its final form. Convinced that President Van Dusen was correct, I decided to do something about it. I believe strongly the two Jobs should be kept separate, and that is why we have four chapters in this book. We need to recognize the many voices in the Joban tradition. Both **Job I** and **Job II** (that is, **The Ancient Folktale of Job** and **The Rebel Job**) are important as we deal with the unthinkable problems and the great joys of our time.

---

6. Hone, *The Voice*, 294.
7. I will explain this in detail in the "Introduction."
8. The two additions being chapter 28 and chapters 32–38.

Abbreviations

AAT	*An American Translation*
AB	Anchor Bible
AML	Ancient Mediterranean Literature
ANET	*Ancient Near Eastern Texts* (Pritchard)
Buber and Rosenzweig	*Die Fünf Bücher der Weisung*
CRST	*The Claremont Ras Shamra Tablets*
BHS	*Biblia Hebraica Stuttgartensia*
HUCA	*Hebrew Union College Annual*
JNES	*Journal of Near Eastern Studies*
KJV	King James Version
LXX	Septuagint
MT	Masoretic Text
NRSV	New Revised Standard Version
PRU V	*Le Palais Royal D'Ugarit, V* (Virolleaud)
RS	Ras Shamra
RSP	*Ras Shamra Parallels* (Fisher and Rummel)
RSV	Revised Standard Version
Tanakh	The Holy Scriptures (JPS)
UL	*Ugaritic Literature* (Gordon)
UT	Ugaritic text
UT	*Ugaritic Textbook* (Gordon)

Introduction[1]

MANY VOICES

The Many Voices of Job contains four chapters, each with a different voice. In chapter 1, we hear the voice of **Job I** as narrated in **The Ancient Folktale of Job**.[2] We learn about his loss, his suffering, his integrity, his interrogation, his repentance, and his restoration. The theological voice emphasizes that God is all-powerful, that he punishes the sinners and rewards the righteous. It stresses the idea of retribution.

In chapter 2, we present **The Rebel Job** (or **Job II**).[3] The voice of the rebel is completely different from the Job of the folktale. God is not all-powerful, and the facts belie the idea of retribution. The evildoers have their wealth and their power; they get along just fine. This rebel does not fear the God of his three opponents, and he would never repent before him. Why? For him this God does not exist even though his shadow continues to haunt and cloud the issue. His is an impatient voice as he speaks for all humans. He is especially convinced of one thing: there is no justice.

Chapter 3 is brief. It presents the poem in Job 28, which I have called, "Where Can Wisdom Be Found?" This beautiful poem comes to us from an even later voice than the poets of **Job I** and **Job II**. Inserted as it is in the middle of **Job I**, it interrupts the narrative of **Job I**, even though it agrees with its point of view.

---

1. This "Introduction" is a special introduction in which I explain the problems we face as we translate, interpret, and present the book of Job to people living centuries after the scribal collections of such stories. There are many detailed general introductions. One of the best is Marvin Pope's in *Job*, XV–LXXXIX. For an interesting history of interpretation as seen in selected readings, see Nahum Glatzer's *The Dimensions of Job*.
2. The folktale is narrated in Job 1–2; 27–31; and 38–42.
3. The rebel's voice is found in Job 3–26.

Introduction

Chapter 4 examines "The Speeches of Elihu" as found in Job 32–37. I have often described this document as a late and extremely critical commentary on **The Rebel Job**. Those who agree with the orthodox theology of the rebel's opponents usually like Elihu; but Elihu is not fair or truthful in his criticism. Edwin Good makes an interesting comment about Elihu: "I find Elihu a pompous, insensitive bore: an opaque thinker and an unattractively self-important character."[4] I would only add that Elihu is also in complete agreement with his cruel God.

Three of these four voices are similar with the same tone, but the rebel's voice is one hundred eighty degrees removed. All of these voices are important, but they are not a quartet with beautiful and pleasing harmony. It is best to listen to them one at a time.

There are undoubtedly more than four voices in the book of Job. Readers will find in Job 1:6–12 and 2:1–8, an interesting account about the sons of the gods presenting themselves before Yahweh. Among these members of the divine court was one with the title of *hassatan*, or "the satan." In my earlier translation of the prologue to **Job I**, I left out "the satan"[5] and his role in the testing of Job. In my view these passages are a later addition, and in the oldest form of the **Job I** traditions it was probably God who "tested" Job. This is the implication of the Epilogue where "the satan" does not appear, and it is much like Genesis 22 where it is God who tests Abraham. There will be more on this idea in the notes to chapter 1, but for now I suggest that "the satan" narrative is a later addition. A later writer with a different voice apparently attempts to blame "the satan" for Job's testing rather than Yahweh. But I silenced this addition and now will turn up the volume. We should listen to this voice as well as the main ones.

In still later times, others have lifted their voices and changed the text to promote their points of view. A good example of this is the parade passage in Job 13:15. First, I will give this famous verse in the King James Version and then I will give my translation:

---

4. Good, *In Turns of Tempest*, 321.

5. Note that this is not "Satan." Good translates "the Prosecutor" (ibid., 51). The use of the proper name Satan is a later development than the book of Job.

Introduction

KJV: Though he slay me, yet will I trust *in him*:
But I will maintain mine own ways before him.

Fisher: So, he will kill me; I have *no hope*.
Yet, I will argue my case to his face.

In my translation, note the last two words of the first line: "*no hope.*" The Hebrew text writes "no," and hence we have "no hope or no trust." But the word "no" in Hebrew sounds like the prepositional phrase "to/in him," and many scribes and readers said that it should be read and understood as such: "yet will I trust *in him.*" The King James Version went along with this way of reading the text and completely changed the voice of the rebel Job to that of **Job I**. We should read what is written.

Perhaps scribes have also eliminated some voices. When a voice is silenced, the proof is difficult to discover, but here is a probable example. In Job 2:11–13, the ancient Job's three friends, Eliphaz, Bildad, and Zophar, come to visit and comfort him. In fact they sit and mourn with him for seven days and seven nights, and no one speaks a word. But we have to wonder: what did they say after the seven days? Both Marvin Pope and H. L. Ginsberg suggest that we have lost a section of this story in which the three friends counseled Job to curse God and die as did Job's wife.[6] This would explain why Yahweh's anger burned against these three friends for their incorrect speech but praised Job in the Epilogue, Job 42. It is important to remember that these three friends cannot be equated with the three opponents of the rebel Job in Job 3–26. Though the opponents have the same names, they present us with the voice of the ancient Job. In fact they are orthodox and speak correctly as did the ancient Job. These three opponents only appear in Job 3–26 and in the introduction to the speeches of Elihu, Job 32. Even though the voices of the original three cannot be recovered, we do have the ancient Job's angry response to them and his wife in Job 27. Whoever silenced them caused a great deal of confusion.

---

6. Pope, *Job*, XXVI and XXXI n. 20.

Introduction

THE DATE OF JOB

Many scholars date the book of Job late. This means after the Babylonian exile or after 539 BCE. It seems obvious, however, that no one really knows the date of this book. We all hope that more information will surface to remedy this problem in the future. So, at the present time most of us try to give our best guess. Marvin Pope says, "The seventh century B.C. seems the best guess for the date of the Dialogue."[7] The Dialogue or **The Rebel Job** is a response to **The Ancient Folktale of Job**, so the folktale came first. In my previous work, I have maintained that **The Ancient Folktale of Job** was known in the eastern Mediterranean world long before there was an Israel. We have Sumerian, Babylonian, and Ugaritic parallels to this folktale.[8] We also know that even among the Babylonians there were some who argued against their doctrine of retribution. In *The Babylonian Theodicy*,[9] the friend argues for this doctrine. He says, "Unless you seek the will of god, what luck have you? / He that bears his god's yoke never lacks food, though it be sparse." But the sufferer disagrees: "I have looked around society, but the evidence is contrary. / The god does not impede the way of a devil."[10]

It seems possible that from the time of David and the beginning of a Jerusalem scribal community, about 1000 BCE, **The Ancient Folktale of Job (Job I)** would have been known, and as usual there would have been some who argued against it as in the Babylonian texts and in **The Rebel Job (Job II)**. However this still does not answer the question of when the book of Job was written. Perhaps **Job I** and the arguments against it were among the oral traditions of the day. But one thing is clear: when it was finally published, **Job II** was buried in the text of **Job I**. In my novel, *The Minority Report: Silenced by Religion*, Keziah tells a likely story about her husband, Jonathan, who is a scribe in The Jerusalem Academy. He is also

---

7. Pope, *Job*, XL.

8. Fisher, *The Rebel Job: Revised*, 8–12. Here I discuss Kramer "'Man and His God'"; Lambert *Babylonian Wisdom Literature*, 33, 45, 46, 49–50, 59; and Nougayrol, "(Juste) Suffrant (R.S. 25.460)."

9. I would not call this text a *theodicy*, because it does not vindicate God's justice in the present or the future. Since we do not have the first line and hence the title for this text, I call it *A Dialogue Between an Orphan, Who Suffers, and His Friend*.

10. Lambert, *Babylonian Wisdom Literature*, 85.

Introduction

the author of **The Rebel Job**. This is a novel, but it does deal with many of the problems that any scribe would face in making public a minority opinion. The prophets, priests, and kings of Israel would not appreciate **The Rebel Job**. For now I am suggesting that an early date for the book of Job is certainly probable.

TRANSLATION PROBLEMS[11]

An old friend, Edward Beutner, was fond of the Italian aphorism, *traddutore traditore*. These two words are not easy to move into English with aphoristic impact, but the general sense is "a translator is a traitor." For the translator it is difficult to select among the several meanings of a word, moreover if the word is known, we can never know if the speaker used the word with a smile or a scowl. The role of a traitor to the text is always close at hand. We can pay attention to the context, however, and try to understand the views of each person or speaker in the story. The separation of the two books, **Job I** and **Job II**, did have an impact upon the translation when certain options presented themselves. One of the best examples of how our translations depend upon our awareness of which Job we are translating is found in Job 30:23a. Since I give this to **Job I**, the translation is: "But I know that you will rescue me [from] death." The rebel Job (in **Job II**) would never say this, and since most of the translations make the mistake of seeing this as **Job II**, regardless of their exact understanding of **Job II**, the translation for them is: "I know that you will return me [to] death." In this case, the prepositions "from" and "to" are not written in the text, and the translator must try to understand who is speaking and thus what preposition fits the context.

Another problem to consider, especially when translating poetry, is the form and style of the reproduced sentence or poem in the target language, in this case English. An extremely literal translation does not work, but at the same time we cannot just come up with a paraphrase that reduces the options of the several meanings implied in the text. Hebrew poetry uses few words and the word order is important. To respect this

---

11. For a detailed discussion of this topic, see Good, *In Turns of Tempest*, 14–40.

Introduction

brevity and order in the English translation does not always produce great English. On this issue we walk a fine line.[12]

Another difference in my translation, when compared to other translations, has to do with tense. Translators do not seem to pay close attention to verbal forms. Is there an imperfect or a perfect in the Hebrew text? Some translators take the easy way and use what seems to fit. Edwin Good says, "I have made excessive use of the present tense in translating, for it seems to me temporally the least precise of the English tenses."[13] When translating, I try to use the correct tense. I also use brackets around added words, and parentheses are used for what I consider parenthetical statements within the text.

THE TWO BOOKS

The question remains: why were these two books merged together as they were? **Job I** is a book that the orthodox believers and the king revered. They knew that a populace that feared God and was obedient would bow before both God and king, and would be easier to control. Since Hebrew tradition (in Judges and Isaiah, for example) contains both promonarchical and antimonarchical traditions, it is not difficult to understand **Job II** as an antimonarchical book. The end result is that the orthodox did manage to hide **Job II** regardless of the reasons why they felt they had to keep it rather than just destroying it outright.[14] They hid it well, and the insertion of the Elihu speeches by the orthodox and the establishment were meant to neutralize **The Rebel Job**.

12. Pope, *Job*, LV.
13. Good, *In Turns of Tempest*, 20.
14. Perhaps too many people liked it.

The Ancient Folktale of Job

INTRODUCTION

There is no doubt that there was an ancient story of Job. In Ezekiel 14:14 and 20, Ezekiel mentions three righteous men: Noah, Danel, and Job. These three ancient sages are noted for their righteousness. Danel is mentioned again in Ezekiel 28 and is noted for his wisdom. This Danel also appears in Ugaritic literature, which predates Israel by at least five hundred years. Ugarit was located on the Mediterranean coast of what we now call Syria, and we have recovered many literary texts from there since its discovery in 1929. Two epics from Ugarit are important for our study of Job. One tells the story of Danel and his son Aqhat and the other one is about Keret. As their stories begin, both of these ancestors have suffered the lost their families.

We start with *The Epic of Aqhat and Danel*. The story begins with Danel participating in a seven-day ritual. It is possible that this ritual is a funeral rite. Danel gives food and drink to the gods, who could be Danel's departed ancestors. On the seventh day the god Baal appears. Baal informs the god El that Danel is now without a son. El blesses Danel, and a perfect son is born to him, and he names him Aqhat. At Ugarit, proper funeral rituals brought such blessings, and the purpose of this was to provide an heir. Later on in the story the goddess Anat has Aqhat killed. Now Danel must find Aqhat's "fat and bone," and he must have a proper burial "in the grave of the gods of the netherworld." Again, these gods are the departed ancestors and kings. Danel has another funeral ritual, and even though we do not have the ending of the story, Danel is probably blessed again and has another son.¹ So it is certain that in this ancient world there were stories of restoration as in the ancient story of Job.

*The Epic of Keret*² makes it clear that Keret has lost his entire family. He no doubt buries them with the usual funeral rites. While weeping for them the god El visits him, giving him instructions as to what he must do, with the help of Baal, to once again have a rightful wife and produce a family to carry on his line. In the story this happens as planned. Again, restoration is yours if you obey.

Mesopotamian parallels to Job also exist, and Lambert discusses these in detail.³ The two most important works are *I Will Praise the Lord of Wisdom* and the so-called *Babylonian Theodicy*. Most of the ideas in **Job I** or the ancient Job and those of the "friends" or opponents in **Job II** or **The Rebel Job**, are well known in Mesopotamia during the second millennium BCE. These parallels show us that an ancient story of Job existed in several forms and was certainly around when David began to rule in Jerusalem about 1000 BCE. Since **Job II** was a response to this old story, it is naturally later.

Most scholars know about this ancient Job legend, and they also know that a great poet, who was at least the author of the dialogue in chapters 3–26, used this legend in some way. But the discussion of the legend (**Job I**) and the dialogue (**Job II**) has usually been cloudy and vague. Is the legend contained only in the prose Prologue and Epilogue? Was the legend edited and expanded when it was put into written form? And what about the dialogue? Does the dialogue give us a second Job and a new set of three friends?

In my recent work on Job,⁴ I have tried to answer these questions. I refer to the ancient Job of the legend as **Job I** and the Job of the dialogue in

---

1. I have dealt with this earlier (Fisher, *Genesis*, 35); and for the complete story see Gordon, "Poetic Legends." 5–34.

2. Keret has also been vocalized by various scholars as Kret, Kuritu, and Kirta.

3. Lambert, *Babylonian Wisdom Literature*, 15–94. For the Sumerian Job motif see Kramer, "Man and His God" 170–82.

4. The Center for Process Studies held a conference on *The Book of Job* in 2007 at the Claremont School of Theology. John B. Cobb Jr. invited four presenters to discuss my work on Job. The work discussed: *Who Hears the Cries of the Innocent?* 2002; *The Minority Report*, 2004; and *The Rebel Job*, 2006. The presenters were: Ziony Zevit, George

chapters 3–26 as **Job II** or **The Rebel Job**. Now, I will explain why I believe the story of the ancient Job in chapters 1 and 2 continues in chapters 27 and 29–31 and is completed in chapters 38–42. The structural pattern of prose plus poetry plus prose is evident as it is in an Egyptian story: *A Dialogue between a Man and His Ba.*

In chapters 1 and 2, the ancient Job is described as a man of integrity. "That man was perfect and upright, one who feared Elohim and avoided evil" (1:1b). He was perfect in that he was complete (Hebrew: *tam*). In Yahweh's conversation with "the satan," it is repeated that Job is perfect and upright (Job 2:3). Job's wife takes up this theme again. "Do you still hold fast to your integrity? Curse Elohim and die" (Job 2:9).

It is well known that the ancient Job is portrayed as a patriarchal figure, and as we said above, Ezekiel 14:14 associates him with Danel (from Ugarit) and Noah. So regardless of one's understanding of the two Jobs and the dating of the two documents, it should not seem strange that the ancient Job's response to his great losses would be that of obedience. We are also told that he did not sin (Job 1:22). After he was afflicted with horrible sores all over his body, his wife said, as mentioned above, "Do you still hold fast to your integrity? Curse Elohim and die" (Job 2:9). Then we are told, "Job did not sin with his lips" (Job 2:10b). Job tells his wife that her speech is foolish, but he does not really answer her question. Does he still hold fast to his integrity? The answer seems to be delayed in the narrative with the arrival of the friends.[5] Job's response to his wife (and to his friends) can be found in 27:1–23 and in 29:1—31:40. Both of these responses are in the form of a *mashal*: "Again Job took up his *mashal*; he said: . . ." The meaning of *mashal* in this context is "*a poetic autobiographical portrait.*"[6] Job uses this portrait to answer his wife's question. He begins with a solemn vow, saying, "I will not put my integrity

---

V. Pixley, John T. Wilcox, and James A. Sanders. We had a lively discussion complete with panelists and an intelligent interactive audience. We did not always agree, but as in **The Rebel Job** the dialogue was great. At the end of the day, I was questioned concerning the narrative flow of **Job I**. This introduction is, in part, my response to that question, and it shows why **Job II** ends with chap. 26.

5. See Pope, *Job*, xxxi. Pope refers to H. L. Ginsberg's view that the three friends might well have joined Job's wife in urging Job to curse God. If so, this accounts for Yahweh's anger against the three friends in the Epilogue. These three friends are not to be equated with the three opponents in the dialogue of **The Rebel Job**.

6. On *mashal* see Johnson, "*Mashal*," 162–69 but especially 165 and 167.

from me. I have maintained my righteousness, and I will not let it go" (27:5b–6a). His response is a resounding yes to his wife's question, but it is not without complaint.

To respond with a *mashal* is to follow the old way; it is to follow the way of Balaam, who in his *mashal* could not curse but only bless, and here Job will not curse. Note the divine names, El and Shaddai in Numbers 24:4 and Job 27: 2.[7] This response in the genre of a *mashal* is a first-person monologue and is not to be confused with the dialogue in 3–26. Yes, some of chapter 27 repeats the voice and the views of the "friends" in the dialogue. This is to be expected, because these "friends" agree with the ancient Job.[8] It is interesting that we were told in chapter 2 that Job did not sin with his lips, and in his response (27:4 and 5) he says:

> My lips will not speak falsehood,
> And my tongue will not utter deceit.
> Deceit would be mine if I should justify you;
> Until I die I will not put my integrity from me.

Job's response is firm. He will not curse God and die. Rather, until the end of his life, he will maintain his integrity, his innocence. I do not think the rebel Job claims such righteousness and integrity. The rebel did make a similar claim in 9:20–24, but this was in an angry response to what Bildad said in 8:20: "El does not reject a perfect (*tam*) person." In chapter 9 the rebel does claim to be innocent, perfect, and complete (*tam*), but such claims are meaningless, because both the innocent (*tam*) and the guilty will be destroyed.

In chapters 29–31 the ancient Job continues to stress his integrity and righteousness.[9] His final words at the end of the second *mashal* are: "The words of Job are complete." Here the word for "complete" is once again Hebrew *tam*. Given this theme in this ancient story, we should re-

---

7. In Numbers 24:15–19 the use of the first person is important to Eissfeldt in his discussion of Balaam; Eissfeldt, *The Old Testament*, 54.

8. Pope, *Job*, 191. Here Pope says that 27:8–23 gives us the point of view of the "friends" and not Job. This is true if you are thinking of the rebel Job, but these views also belong to the Job of **Job I**.

9. See 29:14 and 31:6.

member that the words of Job are not only finished but are also complete, perfect, and speak of his integrity.[10]

After Job's final words the story moves on to the final segment in chapters 38–42: Yahweh's interrogation from the whirlwind, the ancient Job's repentance, and restoration as seen in the Epilogue.

TRANSLATION: THE ANCIENT FOLKTALE OF JOB

1 ¹There was a man in the land of Uz; his name was Job.[11] That man was perfect and upright, one who feared Elohim and avoided evil. ²Seven sons and three daughters were born to him. ³His property included seven thousand sheep, three thousand camels, five hundred yoke of oxen, five hundred donkeys, and many servants. That man was greater than any of the Bene-qedem.[12]

⁴His sons would go and make a feast in the house of each one on his day.[13] They would send and invite their three sisters to eat and drink with them. ⁵When the days of the feast had gone around, Job would send [a message]; he would sanctify them. He would rise early in the morning; he would offer burnt offerings, as many as all of them, for Job said: "Perhaps my children have sinned and cursed Elohim in their heart."[14] Thus would Job do all the time.

---

10. At the beginning of this *mashal* there is an attribution: "Again Job took up his *mashal*." So the final words ("The words of Job are complete") amount to double attribution that is common in Egyptian narrative.

11. On the name Job see Pope, *Job*, 6. Here Pope refers to W. F. Albright's view on the meaning of "Job," Hebrew ʿiyyôb. He says that it means, "Where is my father?" The answer to such a "where" question is, "my father is dead." You will see a discussion of this in chapter 2, "The Rebel Job." Note Job 14:10. Was Job an orphan?

12. Or "Easterners." Qedem is the final destination of the protagonist in the Egyptian story of *Sinuhe*.

13. "His day" is his birthday.

14. "Heart" is also translated "mind" depending on the context. This I do in 1:7.

The Many Voices of Job

⁶*One day* the sons of the gods came and stationed themselves before Yahweh; moreover the *satan*[15] came with them. ⁷Yahweh said to the *satan*, "Where did you come from?"[16]

The *satan* answered Yahweh; he said, "From roving the earth and moving about in the [earth].

⁸Yahweh said to the *satan*, "Have you thought about my servant Job? There is none like him on the earth, a perfect and upright man who fears Elohim[17] and avoids evil."

⁹The *satan* answered Yahweh; he said, "Does Job fear Elohim for no reason? ¹⁰Have you not made a hedge for him, for his house, and for everything he has? From every side you have blessed the work of his hands, and his property[18] has increased on the earth. ¹¹But just put out your hand and touch all that he has, and he will curse you to your face."

¹²Yahweh said to the *satan*, "Here, all he has is in your hand, only do not put your hand on him."

The *satan* went out from the presence of Yahweh.

¹³*One day* his sons and his daughters were eating and were drinking wine in the house of their firstborn brother.

¹⁴A messenger came to Job; he said:

> The oxen were plowing,
> And the donkeys were grazing beside them.
> ¹⁵The Sabeans attacked; they took them,
> And they devoured the plowmen with the sword.
> I have escaped, only I alone, to tell you.

¹⁶This one was still speaking, and another one came; he said:

> The fire of Elohim[19] fell from the heavens.
> It burned the flocks and the shepherds.
> It consumed them.
> I have escaped, only I alone, to tell you.

---

15. "The *satan*" is not the later Satan of Jewish and Christian tradition. The *satan* is a member of the divine court and is sometimes thought to be an adversary, prosecutor, or even a spy (see Pope, *Job*, 10).

16. This is the ubiquitous question and the first question that is asked of travelers in Egyptian stories.

17. "A man who fears God/Elohim" is religious.

18. Or one could say, "his herds have burst forth upon the earth."

19. The "fire of Elohim" means "lightning."

¹⁷This one was still speaking, and another one came; he said:
> The Chaldeans formed three columns;
> They raided the camels; they took them.
> And they devoured the servants with the sword.
> I have escaped, only I alone, to tell you.

¹⁸This one was still speaking, and another one came; he said:
> Your sons and your daughters
> Were eating and drinking wine
> In the house of their firstborn brother,
> ¹⁹When a great wind came from across the wilderness.
> It struck the four corners of the house.
> It fell upon the young people. They died.
> I have escaped, only I alone, to tell you.

²⁰Job got up; he tore his robe; he shaved his head; he fell to the ground; he worshiped.

²¹He said:
> "Naked I came out from the womb of my mother,
> And naked I shall return there.[20]
> Yahweh gave, and Yahweh took away.
> Blessed be the name of Yahweh."

²²From all of this, Job did not sin; he did not cast reproach on Elohim.

2 ¹*One day* the sons of the gods came and stationed themselves before Yahweh; moreover the *satan* came with them to station himself before Yahweh. ²Yahweh said to the *satan*, "Where did you come from?"

The *satan* answered Yahweh; he said, "From roving the earth and moving about in the [earth]."

³Yahweh said to the *satan*, "Have you thought about my servant Job? There is none like him on the earth, a perfect and upright man, who fears Elohim and avoids evil; he still maintains his integrity, though you turned me against him—to ruin him for no reason."[21]

---

20. "There" refers to a returning to the earth, a final womb.

21. In 1:9 the *satan* asks the question, "Does Job fear Elohim for no reason?" Here the same word (in Hebrew and English) is used. Yahweh is throwing it back to the *satan*.

The Ancient Folktale of Job

⁴The *satan* answered Yahweh; he said, "Skin for skin! All that this man has, he will give for his being. ⁵But just put out your hand and touch his bone and flesh, and he will curse you to your face."²²

⁶Yahweh said to the *satan*, Here, he is in your hand but preserve his being."

⁷The *satan* went out from the presence of Yahweh. He struck Job with horrible boils from the sole of his foot to his pate.

⁸[Job]²³ took a potsherd with which to scrape himself, and he was the one who sat in the midst of the ashes. ⁹His wife said to him, "Do you still hold fast to your integrity? Curse Elohim and die."

¹⁰[Job] said to her, "You speak as one of the foolish women talk. Should we, indeed, accept the good from the gods, and not accept the evil?" From all of this, Job did not sin with his lips.

¹¹The three friends of Job heard of all this evil that had come upon him. They came each from his place, Eliphaz the Temanite, Bildad the Shuhite, and Zophar the Naamathite. They arranged together to go to console him and to comfort him. ¹²They lifted up their eyes from afar; they did not recognize him; they lifted up their voices; they wept. Each one tore his robe. They threw dust heavenward upon their heads. ¹³They sat with him on the earth, seven days and seven nights. No one spoke a word to him for they saw that the suffering was very great.

27¹ Again²⁴ Job took up his *mashal*;²⁵ he said:

² [As] El²⁶ lives, he has taken away my justice;
And Shaddai,²⁷ he has embittered my soul.²⁸

---

22. Even as Yahweh goes back to their first conversation in 1:9, so the *satan* goes back to his response in 1:10-11. It is helpful to note his use of the preposition *beʿad* in the sense of "for" in 1:10 and 2:4. This preposition is difficult in both verses, but I have translated "for" consistently.

23. I have replaced the pronoun in the verbal form with "Job."

24. Job now continues his speech against his wife's suggestion "to curse Elohim and die," but he is also speaking to his three friends who probably agreed with his wife.

25. The Hebrew word *mashal* in this context means "*a poetic autobiographical portrait.*" This is different from the dialogue in chaps. 3-26.

26. *El.* This is an ancient name for god and it means "god." At Ugarit El was the head of the pantheon. This is Job's vow.

27. *Shaddai.* Here is another name for god.

28. Our ancient Job has already said that one should be able to accept both good and

3 But while my breath is in me,
   And the wind of Eloah[29] is in my nostrils,
4 My lips will not speak falsehood,[30]
   And my tongue will not utter deceit.
5 Deceit would be mine if I should justify you;[31]
   Until I die I will not put my integrity from me.
6 I have maintained my righteousness, and I will not let it go.
   My heart does not reproach any of my days.
7 May my enemy be as [the] wicked
   And my opponent as the unjust.
8 For what hope has the irreligious when he is cut off,
   When Eloah takes away his being?[32]
9 Will El hear his cry,
   When trouble comes upon him?
10 Or will he delight in Shaddai,
   Will he call to Eloah at all times?
11 I will teach you concerning the power of El;[33]
   What is with Shaddai I will not conceal.
12 Yes you, all of you, have seen,
   And why is it that you create utter futility?[34]
13 This is [the] lot of [the] wicked human from El,
   And [the] inheritance that oppressors receive from Shaddai.

---

evil from Elohim (2:10). Job is repeating himself here, and he is still speaking to the foolishness of his wife and his three friends. We must remember that this Job is orthodox.

29. *Eloah.* This is a singular form of Elohim or "gods"

30. Compare this line with 2:10.

31. It is important to remember that Job is speaking to his wife and friends who want him to "curse" God.

32. Marvin Pope gives vv. 8–23 to "part of Zophar's missing speech." He also says "These verses present the point of view of the friends and cannot be attributed to Job" (Pope, *Job*, 191). In the first place there may not be a missing speech, but more to the point, Pope is talking about **Job II** and his friends. In v. 8 we are dealing with **Job I**, and this is his view, which would be like Zophar's in **Job II**. Again and again we confuse the two Jobs and the two sets of friends.

33. "Power" is a translation of the word "hand." One could also say, "I will teach you [what] is in the hand of El."

34. Once again Job is speaking to his wife and friends. Their response was and is futile.

The Many Voices of Job

14 If his children are many, they are for the sword,
   And his offspring will not have enough food.
15 His posterity will be buried with Mot,[35]
   And his widows will not weep.
16 Though he heaps up silver like dirt,
   And like clay provides garments,[36]
17 He may provide, but the righteous will wear [it],
   And [the piles of] silver, [the] innocent will share [it].
18 He has built like a watchman[37] his house,
   And like [the] hut [that] the guard made.
19 He lies down rich but not again;
   His eyes were open, but he was gone.
20 Terrors overwhelm him like the water;
   [In the] night, a storm snatched him away.
21 The east wind picks him up, and he goes,
   And it whirls him from his place.
22 And it buffets him without compassion;
   From its power he certainly is pushed.
23 It claps its palms at him,
   And blows him from his place.[38]

29 1 **Again Job took up his *mashal*;[39] he said:**
2 O that I were as in the months of old;[40]
   As in [the] days when Eloah guarded me;
3 When his lamp shone over my head,
   [And] by his light I walked [in] darkness;

---

35. Mot is the god of death, and to be buried with Mot is not to be buried in the family tomb where the dead are remembered and cared for.

36. This traditional word pair "dust and clay" I translate "dirt and clay." It is difficult to know exactly what is meant and why these two words are used in this context. This is not the case in Job 4:19 and 10:9 (for this see **Job II**). Perhaps the silver and garments, to the rich, are not of great value and are like dirt and clay.

37. Here I follow Marvin Pope's suggestion (*Job*, 193).

38. Again this is the orthodox view of **Job I**. The rich and the powerful will be judged and do not forget it.

39. For the meaning of *mashal* see the note for 27:1.

40. A more literal translation would be something like: "Who could give to me as in [the] months of old?"

4 Even as I was in the autumn of my days,
   When the counsel of Eloah was over my tent,
5 When Shaddai was still with me,
   When my young ones[41] were around me;
6 When my steps were bathed in cream,
   And [the] cliff poured out for me streams of oil.[42]
7 When I went out [the] gate from [the] city,
   I was taking my seat in the square.
8 [The] young men saw me and hid,
   And [the] old men rose up and stood.
9 Princes held back words,
   And they put a hand[43] to their mouth;
10 [The] voices of the leaders were hushed,
   And their tongues were stuck to their palates.
11 When [the] ear heard, it blessed me;
   When [the] eye saw, it testified for me.
12 For I rescued the poor, who cried out
   And [the] orphan, who had no helper.
13 [The] blessing of the destitute was always coming to me,
   And the heart of [the] widow I was always making glad.[44]
14 I put on righteousness; it clothed me;
   Like a robe and a turban was my justice.[45]
15 Eyes, I was to [the] blind,
   And feet to [the] lame was I.
16 I was a father to the needy,
   And I investigated the dispute I did not know.
17 I broke the fangs of the wicked,
   And from his teeth I threw out [the] prey.

---

41. Today with inclusive language in mind, this is the preferred translation. However, the word actually means "boy," "servant," or even a "soldier." See v. 8 below. However, the above translation goes along with Job 1:19.

42. These lines with "cream" and "oil" symbolize plenty.

43. Actually "they put a palm to their mouth."

44. This is the traditional task of the righteous king, which is to care for the poor, the orphan, the destitute, and the widow.

45. The rebel in **Job II** would not make such claims.

18 I thought, "I shall expire within my home,[46]
And like sand I shall multiply my days;
19 My root is one spreading to water,
And dew is lying on my branches.
20 My glory is new within me,
And my bow becomes better in my hand.
21 They listened to me and waited,
And they kept silent for my counsel;
22 After my speech, they would not answer,
And upon them my word would continue to drip.[47]
23 They waited for me like the rain,
And they opened their mouths for the late rain.
24 I smiled at them; they could not believe [it],
Yet the light of my face they could not dismiss.
25 I would decide their course, and I would sit [as] chief,
And I would dwell as king among the troops,
Like one who comforts mourners.

30 1 *And now,*[48] they have laughed at me,
Those who are younger than I,
Whose fathers I would have refused
To put with the dogs of my flock.
2 So, the strength of their hands, for what [use] is it to me?
Among them vigor has perished.
3 From want and from famine they are unproductive,
The emaciated[49] ones of [the] desert,
The dark waste and wasteland;
4 They pluck saltwort from the bush
And broom root for their food.
5 From [the] community they are driven;
They shout at them like the thief.

46. "Home." The Hebrew word means "nest."
47. In light of the context, there is no need to add to our text "like dew."
48. *And now*. This expression is used in vv. 1, 9, and 16. It is used to indicate a new paragraph in Ugaritic and Hebrew letters. There is an abrupt change from Job's greatness in chap. 29 to his nothingness in chap. 30. This was difficult to bear.
49. Here I depend on Arabic.

The Ancient Folktale of Job

6 To live in dreadful wadis,
   [In] caves [in the] dirt and rocks.
7 Among the bushes they bray;
   Under the scrub they huddle.
8 Sons of a fool, moreover sons of no name,
   They were scourged from the earth.

9 *And now*, I have become their song;
   I have become for them a word.[50]
10 They have detested me; they have stayed far from me,
   And from my face they have not refrained [their] spit,
11 Because my cord[51] was loosened, it afflicted me,
   And they cast off restraint[52] before me.
12 On [the] right a gang rises up;
   They shot my feet;
   They built up their roads of destruction against me.
13 They broke up my path;
   They profit from my destruction;
   [There is] no help from them,
14 For they come through a wide breach;
   Beneath [the] devastation they rolled on.
15 Terrors fell upon me,
   Pursuing like the wind my dignity,
   And like a cloud my prosperity has passed.

16 *And now*, my soul pours itself out against me;[53]
   Days of affliction seize me.
17 [At] night my bones were torn from me,
   And my gnawers never lie down.

---

50. In this verse the song is a mocking song, and the word is a byword.

51. Perhaps this word "cord" should be compared to "belt." See the note for Job 12:18–21 in chapter 2 of this book.

52. Here I follow others with some misgivings. The word means "bridle."

53. Again I am reminded of the Egyptian story: *A Dialogue between a Man and His Ba*.

13

18 With violence my garment is changed;
   By the neck of my tunic it [54] girds me.[55]
19 He has cast me into [the] slick clay;
   I have become as slime and ashes.
20 I cry to you, but you do not answer me;
   I stood [before you]; you considered me.
21 You are changing to one who is cruel to me;
   With your strong[56] hand you will assault me.
22 You will lift me up [and] mount me on [the] wind;
   You will scatter me [in] a storm.[57]
23 But I know you will rescue me [from] Mot[58]
   And [from the] house of assembly for all living.[59]
24 Surely one does not turn [his] hand against [those] in ruins,
   If in his disaster there is a cry for help for [the women].[60]
25 Did I not weep during difficult days,
   When my being grieved for [the] poor?
26 But when I hoped for good, evil came;
   I expected light; darkness came.

54. It = the garment.

55. This verse is difficult, but I proceed with the assumption that the garment has been torn to shreds and binds him. He is tied up.

56. Or literally "bone."

57. This translation is only a guess.

58. Mot is the god of death at Ugarit. Most translations understand this in an opposite way. "I know that you will bring/return me to death." This might be a possible translation if we were dealing with the rebel Job, but this is not the case. The ancient Job thinks, in spite of all the problems, Elohim will rescue him. It is the prepositions that always give us problems, and here they are only implied. Is it "to" or "from?" In PRU V, 81, there is a letter from the King of Tyre to the King of Ugarit (RS 18.31 or UT 2059). In this letter the King of Tyre reports that a ship from Ugarit was caught in a mighty storm. The sailors were doomed, but he rescued them. He says, ". . . and all of them, from the grip (*bd*) of / the Master of Death (*rb.tmtt*), I took, / and I rescued them" (lines 21–23). In line 23 the verb for "rescue" is identical with the verb in our Job text with the basic meaning of "return."

59. This house will be the home of the living when they die. Also this verse needs to be seen in the light of Elihu's first speech, Job 33:18–30. For the opposite point of view see in **The Rebel Job** 9:31 and 17:13–14.

60. The Hebrew text reads "for them," but it is feminine plural. This verse is very difficult, and this translation is a guess.

27 My bowels have been made to boil,
And they have not been silent.
The days of my misery confronted me.
28 I am the one who walked in gloom with no sun;
I stood in the assembly crying for help.
29 I have been a brother to jackals,
And a companion to ostrich's daughters.
30 My skin has become black upon me,
And my bones are burnt from heat.
31 My harp has been for mourning,
And my flute for the sound of those who weep.

31 1 I made a covenant with my eyes,
And how could I stare lustfully at a virgin.[61]
2 And what is the portion of Eloah from above,
And the inheritance of Shaddai from on high?
3 Is it not disaster for [the] evil,
And calamity for those who do evil?[62]
4 Does he not see my ways
And number all my steps?
5 If I have walked with [the] worthless,
My foot has hurried to deceit;
6 Let him weigh me on just scales,
And let Eloah know my integrity.
7 If my step strays from the way,
Or my heart has gone after my eyes,
Or a stain has remained on my palms,
8 May I sow and another eat,
And my offspring be uprooted.
9 If my heart has been enticed by a woman,[63]
And I have lain in wait at my neighbor's door

---

61. This could also be "a young maiden." Or should this be "The Virgin" such as the Virgin Anat? In other words he will not worship a goddess. This is a hard question.

62. The answer to this question is an obvious yes. This is the ancient Job's orthodox position, and the position of the three "friends" in **The Rebel Job (Job II)**.

63. There is an interesting double entendre for both the subject and the verb. "Heart" also means "mind" and "entice" also means to be "simple" (open-minded!). Compare this with v. 27 below.

The Many Voices of Job

10 May my wife grind for another,
And may others kneel over her!

11 For that was a crime,
And it is a crime to be prosecuted.

12 For that is a fire that devours to Abaddon,[64]
And it destroys from all my increase.

13 If I despise the justice of my male or female slave,
When they have a complaint against me,

14 What will I do when El rises,
Or when he visits, what will I answer him?

15 Did not he who made me in the belly make him?[65]
One[66] formed us in the womb.

16 If I withhold from [the] pleasure of [the] poor,
Or cause [the] eyes of [the] widow to fail,

17 Or I eat my bread alone,
And [the] orphan did not eat from it, . . . ;[67]

18 For from my youth he raised me as a father,
And since the belly of my mother, I always guide her.

19 If I see one who is perishing from lack of clothing,
And there is no covering for the needy;

20 If his loins did not bless me,
And from the fleece of my sheep he warms himself;

21 If I have raised my hand against the orphan,
When I see my help in the gate;

22 May my shoulder drop from its socket,
And my lower arm be broken from my upper arm.

23 For the disaster of El is a dread for me,
And because of his majesty I am disabled.

64. See 26:6 in **The Rebel Job** for a parallel with Sheol.

65. The pronoun "him" refers to the slave. The NRSV changes "him' to "them," but the slave has already been defined as male or female. This is one of the better things the ancient Job says, but it does not necessarily mean that Job and slaves are equal.

66. "One" is a name for God. See **The Rebel Job** 14:1 and 23:13. Most gods in this ancient culture had numerical names. In Egypt Amon-Re is "One," but see Gordon, "His Name is 'One,'" where he translates Zechariah 14:9 "on that day Yahweh will be one, and his name 'One.'"

67. Something seems to be missing. We need to conclude with something like ". . . , this would be horrible."

24 If I made gold my confidence[68]
   Or called fine gold my security,
25 If I rejoice when my wealth is great
   Or when my hand discovered plenty,
26 If I see the light when it shines
   Or the moon when it moves in splendor,
27 [If] in the secret place my heart was enticed,[69]
   [And] my hand kissed from my mouth,[70]
28 That too would have been a crime to be prosecuted,
   For I would have deceived El from above.
29 If I rejoice at my foe's ruin,
   Or was thrilled when evil found him,
30 I have not allowed my palate to sin,
   By asking [for] his life with a curse.
31 Indeed, the men of my tent said,
   "Who gives from his meat?"[71]
   Are we not sated?"
32 The stranger does not lodge in the street;
   My door to the wayfarer I open.
33 If I hid my transgressions like Adam,
   Hiding my guilt in my bosom,
34 Because I dread [the] great crowd,
   And [the] contempt of [the] families terrifies me,
   I would be silent; I would not go out [the] door.[72]
35 O that someone would listen to me!
   Here is my signature; let Shaddai answer me,
   And [send the] document my opponent has written.[73]
36 Indeed, I would carry it upon my shoulder;
   I would bind it upon me [like] a crown.

---

68. This may be a pun, because this word can also mean "stupidity."
69. In this line the subject and the verb are the same as in v. 9.
70. This probably describes the throwing of a kiss to the moon as an act of worship.
71. The answer is Job.
72. The rebel Job (in chapters 3–26) would never have uttered these self-curses (also he would never have agreed with v. 3). This chapter belongs to **The Ancient Story of Job**.
73. The opponent is God. This seems to be a request for acquittal rather than a trial.

37 I would tell him the number of my steps;
   Like a prince I would approach him.
38 If my land cries out against me,
   And its furrows weep together,
39 If I ate its yield without silver,[74]
   Or caused to expire the life of its tenants,
40 Instead of wheat, let thorns grow up
   And instead of barley, weeds.

The words of Job are complete.[75]

38 1 **Yahweh answered Job from the whirlwind; he said:**
2 Who is this who darkens counsel
   With words without knowledge?
3 Gird up your loins like a hero;
   I will ask you, and you tell me.[76]

4 Where were you when I founded [the] earth?
   Tell if you have understanding.
5 Who fixed its measurements? Surely you know!
   Or who stretched over it a line?
6 Upon what were its pedestals sunk,
   Or who laid its cornerstone,
7 While the morning stars sang together,
   [And the] sons of [the] gods shouted for joy?
8 [Who[77]] shut in the sea with doors,
   [When] in its bursting forth, it came out from [the] womb?
9 When I made a cloud its garment
   And a thick cloud its swaddling-band,

---

74. That is, without paying for it. In this last section (vv. 38–40), we have another self-curse.

75. The words of the ancient Job are finished, complete, and perfect. I understand this on the basis of the Hebrew *tam*, and indeed this Job is a man of "integrity." Now it is time for Yahweh to respond.

76. This sounds like it is God who takes Job to court.

77. Here "who" has some support from the ancient versions and from the Qumran Targum (one of the Dead Sea Scrolls).

10 I extended[78] my limits upon it;
   I set up a bar and doors.
11 I said, "You may come to here but no farther,
   And here your majestic waves halt."[79]
12 Have you ever commanded a morning,
   [And] caused Dawn[80] to know its place,
13 To seize the corners of the earth,
   Shaking the wicked out of it?
14 It[81] changes like clay of a seal,
   And they[82] stand out like a garment,[83]
15 And their[84] light is withheld from the wicked,
   And the upraised arm is broken.
16 Have you entered the springs of Yamm,[85]
   Or walked on the mountains of Tehom?
17 Have the gates of Mot been revealed to you,
   Or can you see the gates of the shadow of Mot?[86]
18 Do you comprehend the breadth of [the] earth?
   Tell, if you have known all of this.
19 Where is the street where light lives,
   And darkness, where is its place?
20 That you may take it to its border,
   And that you may understand the paths to its house.

---

78. The Hebrew word for "extended" actually means, "to break." I think that when the sea broke forth, God once more had to control it. However, this time he broke the old limits and extended them, and now they are fixed.

79. For "halt" I follow Pope and his suggestion of the parallel with UT 68:27 (*Job*, 294).

80. Dawn is a divine being, and one of its activities is to expose the wicked as detailed in v. 13. For the story of *The Birth of the Gods (Dawn and Dusk)* see Gordon, *Ugaritic Literature*, 57–62.

81. This refers to the earth.

82. Referring to the various forms.

83. The light of Dawn causes the various forms to be seen. Granted "like a garment" is difficult.

84. This "light" must be that of Dawn and other morning stars. This sounds like more orthodox theology coming straight from God.

85. Yamm is the name of the god of the "Sea," and Tehom (related to the Babylonian goddess Ti'amat) is the name of the "Deep."

86. Mot is the god of death.

21 You have known, for you were about to be born then,
   And the number of your days is great.
22 Have you entered the treasuries of snow,
   Or do you see the treasuries of hail,
23 Which I have reserved for a time of trouble,
   For a day of attack and war?
24 Where is the road to where light shines forth,
   [Where the] east [wind] scatters over [the] earth?
25 Who cut a channel for the torrent,
   And a path for the thunderstorms,
26 To bring rain on no-man's land,[87]
   A wilderness with no human in it,
27 To satisfy waste and desolation,
   And to sprout grass [in its] place?
28 Does the rain have a father,
   Or who brought forth the drops of dew?
29 From whose belly came forth the ice,
   [The] frost of heaven, who bore it?
30 Like stone [the] waters freeze,
   And the surface of Tehom is frozen.
31 Can you bind the fetters of Pleiades,
   Or loosen the bands of Orion?
32 Can you lead out Mazzarot[88] in its season,
   Or can you guide them, [the] Bear with her cubs?
33 Do you know the statutes of [the] heavens,
   Or can you establish [their] rule on the earth?
34 Can you raise your voice to the cloud,
   And a flood of waters covers you?[89]
35 Can you cast out [bolts of] lightning, and they go,
   And they say to you, 'here we are'?

---

87. This line is a good one, and I took it from Pope (*Job*, 289).

88. See the note for Job 9:9 (in **The Rebel Job**) for these constellations. We do not know much about Mazzarot, but it could be equated with the "chambers of Teman" (or the south) in 9:9.

89. This phrase in 34b is exactly the same as in 22:11b in **The Rebel Job**. I have left it as it was in 22:11b, but in this context it could be changed just a bit.

The Ancient Folktale of Job

36 Who put wisdom in Thoth,
   Or who gave Sekwi understanding?[90]
37 Who can count clouds with wisdom,
   And who tilts [the] waterskins of [the] heavens?
38 When dust flows into the clod,
   And clods cling together?
39 Do you hunt prey for a lioness,
   And can you satisfy [the] appetite of young lions,
40 When they crouch in dens,
   They stay in their cover, [their] lair?
41 Who provides for the raven its food,
   When its young cry to El?
   They wander about for lack of food.

39 1 Do you know the birth season of the mountain goats,
   Do you watch [the] doe giving birth,
2 Do you count [the] months they fulfill,
   Do you know the season they give birth?
3 They crouch and push out their offspring;
   They deliver their young.
4 Their offspring are healthy; they grow up in the open;
   They leave and do not return to them.
5 Who set the wild ass free,
   And who loosed [the] bonds of [the] swift ass?
6 Whose home I have made [the] wilderness
   And whose dwelling [the] salt flats.
7 He[91] laughs at [the] uproar of [the] city;
   He does not hear [the] shouts of [the] driver.
8 He roams the hills [for] his pasture,
   And he searches after anything green.
9 Will [the] wild ox consent to serve you,
   Or will he spend the night by your crib?

---

90. Marvin Pope has a full explanation of these two Egyptian gods (*Job*, 302). Thoth is the God of writing and wisdom; Sekwi (in Coptic *souchi*) might be the Coptic name for Mercury.

91. The NRSV is a translation that uses "inclusive" language. It avoids words like father, son, his, and him. And yet it objectifies all of the other animals. In this verse "he" becomes "it." This was changed from the RSV.

10 Can you hold [the] wild ox in [the] furrow [with] his rope,
   Or will he harrow the valleys after you?
11 Can you rely on him because of his great strength;
   Can you leave your labor to him?
12 Can you trust in him that he will return,
   [That] he will gather your grain [for] your threshing floor?
13 [The] wing of the ostrich is joyful,
   Even if her pinions lack feathers.[92]
14 But she leaves her eggs on the earth,
   And on the dirt she warms them.
15 She has forgotten that a foot might crush [them],
   And a wild beast might trample [them].[93]
16 [The male] was cruel to her offspring as if they were not hers;
   Her labor was in vain without concern.
17 For Eloah deprived her of wisdom,
   And has not given her understanding.
18 When on the heights she flaps [her wings];
   She laughs at [the] horse and his rider.[94]
19 Do you give the horse strength,
   [Or] clothe his neck [with] a mane?
20 Do you make him leap like the locust,
   His majestic snort a terror?
21 He[95] paws with force and exults with strength;
   He goes forth to meet [the] battle.
22 He laughs at fear, and he is not terrified,
   And he does not turn back from the sword.
23 Upon him [the] quiver rattles,
   The blade of [the] spear and [the] javelin.
24 With shaking and excitement he swallows the earth,[96]
   He cannot remain still at [the] blast of [the] horn.

---

92. This is only a guess. I am following Pope (*Job*, 308–9).
93. The Hebrew has "her," but I have changed this to "them."
94. The ostrich is thought to be stupid but is faster than a horse.
95. Hebrew has "they."
96. This expression "swallows the earth" means that the horse is running fast.

The Ancient Folktale of Job

25 At the sound of [the] horn he says, "Aha!"
And from afar he smells [the] battle,
The thunder of the captains and shouting.
26 Does [the] raptor fly by your understanding,
Spreads his wings to [the] south?
27 Will [the] eagle soar at your command,
And will [the] vulture build his nest on high?[97]
28 He dwells [on the] cliff,
And he lodges on [the] pointed rock and [the] stronghold.
29 From there he searches for food;
From afar his eyes can see.
30 And his young ones drink blood,
And where the slain are, there he is.

40 1 **Yahweh answered Job; he said:**
2 "Will [the] fault-finder argue with Shaddai?
He who reproves Eloah, let him answer."
3 **Job answered Yahweh; he said:**
4 "Oh, I am small, how can I answer you?
My hand I put to my mouth.
5 I have spoken once, and I will not answer,
Twice, but not again."
6 **Yahweh answered Job from [the] whirlwind; he said:**
7 Gird up your loins like a hero;
I will ask you, and you will tell me.[98]
8 Would you even destroy my justice?
Would you make me guilty that you may be righteous?
9 Or have you an arm like El's?[99]
Or can you thunder with a voice like his?
10 Deck yourself now [with] majesty and eminence,
And you will be clothed with glory and splendor.

---

97. For this see Pope (*Job*, 314). Pope's use of the Qumran Targum is helpful.

98. Verses 6 and 7 are parallel with 38:1 and 3.

99. Here "arm" is a symbol of power. If Job had such power, he could do all of the following things as listed in vv. 10–13.

The Many Voices of Job

11 Scatter the outbursts of your anger,
    And stare at every proud one and bring him low.
12 Stare at every proud one; humble him;
    Cast down the wicked where they stand.
13 Bury them in the netherworld together;
    Hide their faces in darkness.[100]
14 And even I would praise you,
    For your right hand can save you.
15 Note now Behemoth,[101]
    Whom I made with you,[102]
    He eats grass like cattle.
16 See his strength in his loins,
    And his might in the muscles of his belly.
17 His tail stands up[103] like a cedar;
    The sinews of his thigh are intertwined.
18 His bones are tubes of bronze;
    His skeleton is like bars of iron.
19 He is the first of the powers[104] of El;
    His maker can bring near his sword.
20 Yes, [the] beasts[105] of the mountains support him,
    And all the creatures of the wild play there.
21 Under the lotus he lies down,
    In a covering of reed and swamp.

---

100. *Darkness.* This is equal to Sheol or the netherworld. The netherworld in the previous line is literally "dust."

101. *Behemoth.* This is another mythological monster like Leviathan. See v. 25 and the note for 3:8 in **The Rebel Job**.

102. God made the mythological monsters and can control them. The human is not the center of all things.

103. Here the verb actually means "delight," and the dictionaries give us a second meaning in order to deal with this verse. However, this is not helpful. Many animals make their tails "stand up" when they are having a "delightful time."

104. *Powers.* The meaning of this word is usually "way." But in 26:14a in **The Rebel Job**, I have translated it as "rule," and it is used in this way in Ugaritic. It could be left as, "He is the first of the ways of El," but what does that mean? Most see this verse and Proverbs 8:22 using "way" as one of God's creative works. It seems that the "Maker" has made the primordial monsters (also Leviathan), and he must also control them.

105. See Pope, *Job*, 325.

The Ancient Folktale of Job

22 [The] lotus give him his shade;
   [The] willows of [the] wadi surround him.
23 When [the] stream pushes, he does not worry;
   He is confident [even] when [the] river burst forth to his mouth.
24 Can one take him by his eyes?
   Can one pierce [his] nose with traps?
25 Can you draw out Leviathan with a hook,
   And press down his tongue with a rope?[106]
26 Can you put a cord through his nose,
   And can you pierce his jaw with a hook?
27 Will he make many pleas to you,
   Or will he speak softly with you?
28 Will he make a covenant with you?
   Will you take him for an eternal slave?
29 Will you play with him like a bird,
   And can you bind him for your girls?
30 Will traders bargain over him,
   Will they divide him among merchants?
31 Can you fill his hide with harpoons,
   And with fish spears his head?
32 Lay your hand on him;
   Remember [the] battle;
   Do not do it again.

41 1 See, his hope is deceptive;[107]
   Moreover, is El cast down at the sight of Him?
2 Is he not fierce when one rouses him?
   So who is he who can take a stand before him?
3 Whoever has confronted me? I will repay
   (Everything under the heavens is mine).
4 Did I not silence his songs
   And heroic deeds? Hayyin prepared it.[108]

106. This verse follows the Hebrew numbering. Some Bibles follow the Greek and Latin numbering at this point and start chapter 41 here.

107. That is, any hope of capturing Leviathan (in this section described as a crocodile?) is wishful thinking.

108. I have followed Marvin Pope in much of this verse (*Job*, 338). Hayyin is the epi-

5 Who has uncovered his outer garment?
  Who can penetrate his double jaws?
6 Who has opened the doors of his face,
  Round about his teeth are terrible.
7 [His] pride is [his] furrows of shields,
  Closed [as] a tight seal;
8 One against the other they touch,
  And wind cannot enter between them;
9 Each one sticks to the other;
  They grasp themselves and cannot be separated.
10 His sneezes flash light,
   And his eyes are like the eyes of dawn.
11 From his mouth torches go forth,
   Sparks of escape.
12 From his nostrils comes smoke,
   Like a boiling and turbulent pot.
13 His breath kindles coals,
   And flame comes forth from his mouth.[109]
14 In his neck dwells strength,
   And before him leaps despair.
15 The dewlaps of his flesh are stuck together,
   Cast on him, immovable.
16 His heart is cast as stone,
   And it is cast as a lower millstone.
17 At his uprising the gods are fearful;
   From breakdowns they are cast down.
18 [The] sword that attacks him does not prevail,
   [Nor] spear, [nor] missile, nor lance.
19 He regards iron as straw;
   Bronze is as a rotten tree.
20 An arrow[110] cannot put him to flight;
   Sling-stones have been changed to chaff on him.

---

thet of Koshar, who in the Ugaritic texts is a great enchanter. He has prepared something to deal with the songs.

109. In vv. 13–17 Leviathan seems to be described as a crocodile; but in vv. 18–21 he is seen as the mythological dragon of flame and fire.

110. Literally "son of a bow."

The Ancient Folktale of Job

21 Clubs are regarded as chaff,
    And he laughs at a quivering javelin.
22 His under parts are sharps of shard;
    He spreads out as a threshing sledge on mud.
23 He makes the deep boil like a caldron;
    He makes Yamm[111] like an ointment pot.
24 After him shines a wake;
    He makes Tehom[112] seem white-haired.
25 There is no one on earth like him,
    One made without fear.
26 He sees all that is lofty;
    He is king over all proud beings.

42 1 **Job answered Yahweh; he said:**
2 I know that you are able to do all things,
   And no purpose can be withheld from you.
3 "Who is this who obscures counsel without knowledge?"[113]
   Indeed I spoke without understanding,
   Wonders beyond me, and I did not know.
4 "Hear now, and I will speak;
   I will question you and you tell me."[114]
5 I heard of you by the hearing of the ear,
   And now my eye has seen you.
6 Therefore I despise, I repent
   In dust and ashes.

7 After[115] Yahweh had spoken these words to Job, Yahweh said to Eliphaz the Temanite:

> My anger is inflamed against you and against your two friends,
> for you have not spoken correctly about me, as did my servant Job.

---

111. That is, "the sea."
112. Or "the deep."
113. This is almost the same as 38:2. Here and in the next verse Job is quoting God.
114. Compare 38:3b and 40:7b.
115. "After" is used to mark a new section. Here we begin the prose Epilogue. Note **The Rebel Job** also begins with this marker in 3:1.

> ⁸So now, take for yourselves seven bulls and seven rams
> and go to my servant Job and sacrifice a burnt offering for yourselves,
> and Job, my servant, will pray for you, for I will lift up his face,
> so that I will not be harsh with you, for you have not spoken correctly
> about me, as did my servant Job.[116]

⁹Eliphaz the Temanite, Bildad the Shuhite, and Zophar the Naamathite went and did as Yahweh had instructed them. Yahweh lifted up the face of Job. ¹⁰Yahweh restored the fortune of Job when he prayed for his friends. Yahweh doubled everything that Job owned.

¹¹All his brothers, all his sisters, and all his former acquaintances came to him. They ate food with him in his house; they consoled and comforted him for all the evil that Yahweh had inflicted on him. They gave him, each one, one *qesitah*[117] and each one, one golden ring.

¹² So, Yahweh blessed the later [days] of Job more than his former [ones]. He had fourteen thousand sheep, six thousand camels, a thousand yoke of oxen, and a thousand donkeys. ¹³He had seven sons and three daughters. ¹⁴He called forth the name of the first, "Jemimah,"[118] and the name of the second, "Keziah,"[119] and the name of the third, "Keren-happuk,"[120] ¹⁵and no women were to be found in all the earth as beautiful as the daughters of Job. Their father gave them an inheritance together with their brothers.[121]

¹⁶After this Job lived one hundred forty years. He saw his children and grandchildren to four generations. ¹⁷ Job died, old and satisfied with life.

---

116. The ancient Job's three friends are not to be confused with the three opponents of the rebel Job in Job 3–26, who said all of the correct things. These three probably joined with the ancient Job's wife and urged Job to curse God. This made Yahweh angry.

117. A unit of exchange. See Genesis 33:19.

118. A dove. Note that the sons were not named.

119. A bow that symbolized the shapeliness of the feminine body.

120. A horn of mascara for the eyes.

121. This is unusual, but it is not unusual to feature the daughters and name them in ancient epic literature. In the Baal mythology from Ugarit we learn that Baal's daughters are: Dewy, Earthy, and Flashy.

The Rebel Job

INTRODUCTION

A *Dialogue between a Man and His Ba*[1] is an important and ancient story in Egyptian literature, and a helpful parallel to **The Rebel Job**. The Egyptian man longs for death and an exit from his miserable existence, but his Ba persuades him not to rush toward death. Rather, his soul counsels him to enjoy the present and love now. **The Rebel Job** has a similar tone, and in Job 3 the rebel longs for some exit from his misery, but the conclusion to the story in Job 26 suggests that instead one should be spending time helping the powerless.

The author of **The Rebel Job** was probably educated in a scribal school in Jerusalem. Most urban centers in the East Mediterranean World had their schools, and I assume that Jerusalem had one. Elsewhere I have even given it a name: The Jerusalem Academy. These schools were well aware of Babylonian and Egyptian literature. Our author was apparently well versed in the ways in which the miseries of this life were usually described, and how others had dealt with this subject in the past.

When I first separated **Job I** and **Job II** in *Who Hears the Cries of the Innocent?*, I wrote an imaginary Prologue and Epilogue for **Job II**. But in this version of **Job II**, which I am calling **The Rebel Job,** I will not attempt to add to the text in any way. It is enough to know that **The Rebel Job** is an angry response to **The Ancient Folktale of Job**. Also it is important to realize that the rebel Job is debating three so-called

---

1. See in Fisher, *Tales from Ancient Egypt*. Ba is the Egyptian word for "soul." This story is dated between 2000 and 1785 BCE.

The Many Voices of Job

"friends," who defend the position and beliefs of **Job I**. We are fortunate the words of the rebel Job have survived, even though they were buried within the old story. This melding of the two books made the book of Job impossible to understand for most readers. In case anyone did understand the words of the rebel Job, the orthodox establishment added the "Speeches of Elihu" at a later time to confuse the arguments of the rebel Job. These speeches are contained in Job 32–37, and I translated them in *The Minority Report*.[2] In chapter 4 of this book, the translation of these speeches is revised, and I have added some notes.

This poem is not an easy read, but it contains some great lines plus the emotions of the rebel pour from these lines. I hope you enjoy it and benefit from its contribution.

THE REBEL JOB

3 1 After this[3] Job opened his mouth; he cursed his day.[4]
  2 **Job answered; he said**:
  3 Perish the day on which I was born;[5]
     The night that said, "A hero is conceived."
  4 That day let it be pitch-black.
     May Eloah[6] from above not find it,
     And light not shine upon it.
  5 May darkness and the shadow of Mot[7] claim it;
     May a cloud settle over it.
     May the deep glooms of day terrify it.

---

2. Fisher, *The Minority Report*, 260–71.

3. "After this" is a marker and transition to a new section, and I think this means that there was a Prologue to **The Rebel Job**, which is now missing. This marker is also used in 42:7 as a transition to the Epilogue. If the royal editors removed the Prologue to **The Rebel Job**, they at the same time connected **The Rebel Job** with the Prologue of **Job I**, and this created confusion.

4. *Day*. This is Job's birthday.

5. The prophet Jeremiah also cursed the day of his birth (20:14–18).

6. *Eloah*. This is a singular form of Elohim or "gods."

7. *Mot*. This is the god of death. Also see v. 21 below. For this expression see Psalm 23:4.

6 That night, may gloom take it.
   Do not count it among the days of the year;
   Within the number of months, it shall not enter.
7 As for that night, may it be barren;
   A joyful sound shall not enter in it.
8 Let those who curse Yamm,[8] damn it,
   Those skilled in arousing Leviathan.[9]
9 May its twilight stars be dark,
   Let it hope for light [where] there is none
   And not see the eyes of dawn,
10 For it did not close the doors of my [mother's] womb,
   Nor hide trouble from my eyes.
11 Why did I not die from [the] womb,
   Or expire [when] I came out from [the] belly?
12 Why did knees[10] receive me,
   Or why breasts that I could nurse?
13 For by now, I would have lain down; I would be quiet;
   I would have been asleep; then I would be at rest,[11]
14 With kings and counselors of the netherworld,
   The ones who built for themselves ruins,[12]

8. *Yamm.* This is the god Yamm, god of the Sea, who plays an important role in the Baal texts from Ugarit. Yamm is a symbol of chaos and must be defeated to restore order in the cosmos. In the Hebrew bible this is also the case. Yahweh defeats the Sea.

9. *Leviathan.* At Ugarit, this is Lotan. Here Leviathan is used as a parallel to Yamm.

10. *Knees.* Whose knees? Either the mother's knees or it could be the father's knees. Note Genesis 30:3, "She (Rachel) said, 'Here is my servant girl, Bilhah; go in to her. / She will bear upon my knees; / I will reproduce, even through her.'" Here, to place the child upon the knees is a form of adoption. Rather than the mother's knees, the knees are those of Rachel. Also, note Genesis 50:23, "Joseph saw the sons of the third [generation] of Ephraim; also the sons of Machir-ben-Manasseh were born on the knees of Joseph."

11. He would be at rest in Sheol or the netherworld.

12. *Ruins.* This has been confusing for many translators. Some think they must translate "rebuild ruins," because kings would not build ruins. Put it this way: when kings build palaces these structures do not last forever. One needs to read again the "Harper's Song from the Tomb of King Intef" (Lichtheim, *Ancient Egyptian Literature*, 196): ". . . / The gods who were before rest in their tombs, / Blessed (5) nobles too are buried in their tombs. / (Yet) those who built tombs, / Their places are gone, / What has become of them? / I have heard the words of Imhotep and Hardedef, / Whose sayings are recited whole. / What of their places? / Their walls have crumbled, / Their places are gone, / As

15 Or with princes who had gold,
   The ones who filled their houses [with] silver.
16 Or [why] was I not like a buried stillborn infant,
   Like babies who never saw light?
17 There[13] rascals cease turmoil,
   And there, the weary are at rest.
18 Together, prisoners are at ease;
   They do not hear the voice of the taskmaster.
19 There small and great[14] are the same,
   And a slave is free from his master.
20 Why does he give light to [the] overworked
   And life to those bitter to the core of being,
21 The ones who wait for Mot,[15] but he is not [there],
   They dig for him more than for treasure,
22 The ones who would rejoice [with] the gods[16] of a grave,[17]
   They would gladly discover a tomb (*qeber*),
23 For a hero (*geber*) whose way is hidden,
   Whom Eloah has protected?[18]
24 In place of my food comes my sighs;
   My groans are poured out as water.
25 That dread I dreaded has come upon me,
   And that which I feared comes to me.
26 I was not at ease,
   And I had no quiet,
   And I had no rest;
   Turmoil engulfed [me].

---

though they had never been!"

13. *There.* This refers to the netherworld.

14. *Small and great.* This expression could be translated "everyone."

15. See v. 5 above.

16. *Gods.* This is not the usual translation, but it is a possible one. The word is usually understood as "to."

17. *Grave.* On this, I follow Pope (*Job*, 32–33).

18. But he is not protected from the test and the injustice of Elohim.

4 ¹ **Eliphaz the Temanite answered; he said:**
² If one attempts a word with you, could you handle it?
But who is able to restrain words?
³ Note! You have instructed many,
And you have strengthened fist-less hands.[19]
⁴ Your words have given support to one who stumbles,
And you have strengthened failing knees.
⁵ Now, when it comes to you, you are impatient.
It touches you; you are terrified.
⁶ Is not your fear[20] your confidence[21]
And the integrity of your ways your hope?
⁷ Remember now, who of the innocent has ever perished,
Or where have the righteous been destroyed?[22]
⁸ As I have seen, those who plow evil
And those who sow trouble, they will reap the same.[23]
⁹ From the breath of Eloah they perish,
And from the wind of his nostrils they are destroyed.
¹⁰ A roar of a lion and a growl of an angry lion,
And teeth of young lions were broken.
¹¹ A lion perishes without prey,
And cubs of a lioness are scattered.[24]

19. When one cannot make a fist, one's hands are weak.
20. That is, "your fear [of God]" or some translate "religion / piety."
21. It is interesting that the Hebrew word for "confidence" can also mean "stupidity."
22. This is a key verse. It describes the basic teaching of the orthodox wisdom school. However, we have Babylonian texts that argue against such a doctrine. In the so-called *Babylonian Theodicy*, the friend argues for this doctrine. He says, "Unless you seek the will of god, what luck have you? / He that bears his god's yoke never lacks food, though it be sparse." But the sufferer disagrees: "I have looked around society, but the evidence is contrary. / The god does not impede the way of a devil." For this discussion see Lambert, *Babylonian Wisdom Literature*, 85. Eliphaz's statement is unbelievable.
23. Most organized religions have adopted Eliphaz' position and also this next statement. There is just a bit of truth in this saying, which has allowed it to become popular, but it also embodies a tragic and handy cover-up. The rebel Job points out many times that the wicked are doing quite well (Job 21:7). "As you sow" was the banner of fundamentalists, who wanted obedient God-fearing followers. This banner was still being waved in the New Testament book of Galatians (see 6:7–10), and strangely, progressives use it today.
24. Verses 10 and 11 are not easy to understand. Apparently the lion is thought of as

The Many Voices of Job

12 A word came to me as a thief [in the night];
  My ear caught a whisper of it.
13 From wild thoughts, from visions of [the] night,
  When deep sleep falls upon humans,
14 Fear fell upon me and trembling,
  And most of my bones were filled with dread,
15 And a wind was blowing over my face;
  The hair of my body was standing up.
16 It was standing still, but I could not discern its appearance.
  A form before my eyes, a whisper, and I heard a voice:
17 "Can a man be made righteous by Eloah?
  Or can a hero be made pure by his Maker?
18 If he cannot trust his servants
  And charges his angels[25] with error,
19 How much the less those who dwell in houses of clay,
  Whose foundation is in the dust,[26]
  Who are crushed before a moth.
20 From morning to evening they are crushed;
  Without accomplishment they perish forever.
21 Is not their tent cord pulled up with them?
  They die and not with wisdom."

5 1 Please call out. Is there anyone to answer you?
  To whom of the holy ones will you turn?[27]
  2 For anger kills a fool,
  And passion slays a simpleton.
  3 I myself have observed a fool taking root;
  Suddenly I cursed his home:

---

evil and thus the lion is punished.

25. *Servants and angels.* Eliphaz refers to these again in 5:1b and in 15:15a. Both times he uses the term "holy ones," and in 15:15a the parallel is complete, "He puts no trust in his holy ones."

26. Here the human's body is once again described as clay, dust, or mud. This parallel was helpful for me in my translation of Genesis 2:7 where the translation is usually "dust." However, I translated it as "clay" ("Yahweh-Elohim formed the human [from] the clay of the ground; . . ."). Also note Job 10:9.

27. See the notes at 4:18 and 15:15.

4 "May his children be far from prosperity;
   May they be oppressed in the gate[28] with no one to help;
5 May the hungry consume his harvest,
   Taking it from the thorns,
   And [the] thirsty gasp for their strength."
6 Yes![29] Evil does not come up from dirt,
   And trouble does not sprout from the ground (*'adamah*).
7 Yes! Humanity (*'adam*) is born for trouble,
   And the sons of Resheph[30] go flying high.
8 But, I myself, I would seek El,[31]
   And before Elohim, I would place my case,
9 Who does great deeds and none can be fathomed,
   Wonders beyond number;
10 Who gives rain upon the face of the earth
   And sends water upon the face of the land;
11 Who raises the lowly on high,
   And mourners are lifted to safety;
12 Who thwarts the plots of [the] crafty,
   And their hands cannot achieve success;
13 Who catches [the] wise in their craftiness,
   And the counsel of twisted minds evaporates.
14 By day, they meet darkness,
   And as in the night, they grope at noon.
15 He saved the needy from the sword of their mouth
   And from the hand of the strong;

---

28. *Gate.* This is the place where court cases were heard. So this righteous "friend" hopes these children will not receive justice.

29. *Yes.* This is like German *Ja.* See my translation of Genesis 4:23–24 where I follow Buber and Rosenzweig ("...Yes, I have slain a man for my wounds... Yes, Cain will be avenged sevenfold...").

30. *Sons of Resheph.* Resheph is a Northwest Semitic god. Pope has an informative note on Resheph in *Job,* 42–43. The children of Resheph could be a poetic image for "sparks" or "flames" as in some translations, or as Pope says it could also refer to Resheph's children flying up "from the netherworld to plague mankind."

31. *El.* This refers to God, or it can be a proper name for God. In the next line we have Elohim, "God." This term is rare in this poem.

16 There was hope for the poor,
   And injustice shut its mouth.[32]
17 Indeed, fortunate is the man whom Eloah corrects;
   Do not reject the discipline of Shaddai.[33]
18 Yes, he injures, and he treats;
   He wounds, and his hands heal.
19 From six troubles he shall rescue you,
   And in seven, evil shall not touch you.
20 In famine, he saves you from death,
   In war, from the wielders of the sword.
21 From [the] scourge of [the] tongue, you shall be hidden,
   And you shall have no fear of destruction that comes.
22 At destruction and at famine you shall laugh,
   And from the beasts of the earth, you shall not fear.
23 For with the stones of the field is your covenant,
   And the wild beasts[34] shall be at peace with you.
24 You shall know that your tent is safe;
   You shall visit your fold and miss nothing.
25 You shall know that your descendants are many;
   Your progeny are like the grass of the earth.
26 You shall come in full vigor to [the] grave,
   As a shock of grain is brought up in its time.
27 Here it is! We have investigated it; it is so!
   Listen and you shall know it for yourself.

6 1 **Job answered; he said**:
   2 O that my anger could be weighed
   And together with my misery be put on the balances,

---

32. In vv. 15 and 16, God is given credit for help. The rebel Job would say that such help has never even been offered. Injustice never shuts its mouth but devours the poor and needy.

33. *Shaddai* is another name for God. These two lines deal with a major theme of the righteous "friends," and suffering is seen as punishment.

34. *Wild beasts.* This is a translation of "beasts of the field." This may be parallel to the "beasts of the earth" in v. 22.

3 Right now, it would be heavier than the sand of the sea.[35]
  Therefore my words cry out vehemently.[36]
4 For the arrows of Shaddai are within me,
  Whose venom my spirit drinks;
  The terrors of Eloah are arrayed against me.
5 Does a wild ass bray over grass?
  Does a bull bellow over his fodder?[37]
6 Can insipid [food] be eaten without salt?
  Or is there flavor in slimy cheese?
7 My being has refused to touch [such things];
  They are like the pollutions of my food.
8 Who will grant that my request will be fulfilled,
  And will Eloah give [me] my hope?[38]
9 May Eloah be pleased; may he crush me;
  May he free his hand and cut me off.
10 That would be my comfort;
   I would revel in unsparing pain,
   For I did not conceal my words[39] [against] the Holy One.
11 What is my strength that I should wait?
   What end that I should prolong my being?
12 Or, is my strength [the] strength of stones?
   Or, is my flesh bronze?
13 Or, has my help vanished within me,
   And has success deserted me?

---

35. See "The Words of Ahiqar," translated by H. L. Ginsberg in *ANET*, 429: "I have lifted sand, and I have carried salt; but there is naught which is heavier than [*rage*]." Also note Proverbs 27:3.

36. Other translations picture Job as being "wild, rash, or reckless." However, the rebel Job is both angry and blunt, and he does not take anything back or make excuses.

37. In other words, Job bellows because he has nothing.

38. His hope is for death (3:11).

39. I read "my words" (without changing the text) instead of "the words of the Holy One." This is also done in the *Tanakh*, 1346. It is probably the case that this Job (the rebel Job) does not even believe in the God of his orthodox "friends," but this God is still around, at least in the arguments of the "friends," and is pummeled by the angry words of the rebel Job.

The Many Voices of Job

14 For the sick [there should be] loyalty from his friend,
    Though he forsakes the fear of Shaddai.[40]
15 My friends have been treacherous like a torrent,
    Like a wadi of torrents, they pass away.[41]
16 [Torrents] are dark with ice;
    Snow covers them.
17 When they should flow, they are dried up;
    When it's hot, they disappear from their place.
18 Stream beds[42] wind their way;
    They go out in the waste, and they perish.
19 The caravans of Tema look;
    The travelers of Sheba hope for them.
20 They are ashamed because of overconfidence;
    They reached the place; they were confounded.
21 Thus you have become nothing.
    You see terror; you are afraid.
22 Have I said, "Give to me,
    From your wealth, pay a bribe for me,
23 Rescue me from [the] hand of an enemy,
    From [the] hand of evil men, redeem me?"
24 Teach me, and I will be silent;
    Where am I wrong? Bring understanding to me.
25 How trenchant are [the] words of the upright!
    How does reproof from you reprove?
26 You think to reprove [with] words,
    But of wind are words of one who despairs.
27 Even over an orphan you would cast lots,
    And you would bargain over your friend.
28 And now be pleased to face me;
    I will not lie to your face.

---

40. The religious (those who fear Shaddai or any other god) have never followed or understood this suggestion on the part of the rebel Job.

41. A flash flood can be dangerous, but when you really need water there is none to be found in a dry wadi.

42. *Stream beds.* The Hebrew word for this is ’orḥot in the MT. In v. 19, I have translated the same Hebrew word as "caravans."

29 Relent! Let there be no injustice!
    Relent! My justification is in this.
30 Is there injustice on my tongue?
    Can my palate not distinguish words?[43]

7 1 Is not warfare[44] [the lot] for man[45] upon earth?
      Are not his days like those of a hireling?
   2 Like a slave who pants for shade,
      And like a hireling who hopes for his wage,
   3 So I have inherited for myself months of emptiness,
      And miserable nights have been apportioned to me.
   4 Whenever I lie down, I always think,
      "When can I get up?"
      But an evening always drags on,
      And I am sated with tossing until dawn.
   5 My flesh is now covered with maggots and lumps of dirt;
      My skin has cracked; it is dripping [pus].
   6 My days are swifter than a weaver's shuttle;[46]
      They are finished[47] without hope.[48]

---

43. *Words.* Here I follow Pope (*Job*, 56), who suggests going with the Ugaritic cognate *hwt*, "word."

44. *Warfare.* Others translate this as "hardship, hard labor, or term of service." Edwin Good translates, "Is not a man conscripted on earth, . . ." (Good, *In Turns of Tempest*, 65). It has to do with forced military service or forced labor. I use the military side of this term, because in the next line and the next verse the issue of "labor is dealt with."

45. *Man.* The NRSV translates this Hebrew word "human being." They do it again in v. 17 and change the singular pronouns to plural forms (also in Psalm 8), as I do (see v. 17 below). In places this is possible, and it must be done in Genesis 1:27, but in this verse, this is a doubtful practice even for the purpose of inclusive language. Here we are reading about the military draft and perhaps forced labor. Job is not being inclusive of all genders here.

46. Again and again Job points to the swiftness of one's days.

47. *Finished.* This is a good translation for here and in Genesis 2:2. It is good, because it covers both meanings of the Hebrew word, i.e. "complete and destroy."

48. *Hope.* Like "finished," the word for hope (*tiqvah*) can be taken in two ways. This is a true double entendre. The Hebrew word means both "hope and thread/cord." Therefore the line (6a) also means, "They are finished (just like the shuttle) without thread." Everything is at an end; the pattern is finished.

7 Remember! My life is as wind;
   My eye will not again see good.[49]
8 The eye that looks for me will not see me;
   Your eye will be on me, but I shall not be there.
9 A cloud is finished;[50] it is gone.
   So is the one who descends to Sheol;
   That one will not ascend;
10 He does not return again to his house;
   Nor will his place know him again.[51]
11 I, moreover, will not restrain my mouth;
   I will speak in the anguish of my spirit;
   I will complain from the bitterness of my soul.[52]
12 Am I Yamm or Tannin,
   That you set a guard over me?[53]
13 Whenever I thought, "My bed will comfort me;
   My couch will ease my complaint,"
14 You would dismay me with dreams,
   Terrify me with visions.
15 My being preferred suffocation,
   Death more than my bones.
16 I despised [my life];[54] I will not live forever.
   Let me be,[55] for my days are a breath.

49. In vv. 7–21 Job is no longer speaking to his so-called friends. Here he speaks to their God, but as we move on, it becomes clear that he does not really believe in such a God.

50. *Finished*. Finished is not a good translation ("evaporated" would be better), but it does allow the reader to note that we are dealing with the same word as we had in 6b above.

51. Once again, this time in vv 9 and 10, we have a parallel with *The Harper's Song* (see the note on 3:14). "Their places are gone, / As though they had never been! / None comes from there,/ To tell of their state,/ To tell of their needs,/ To calm our hearts,/ Until we go where they have gone!" (Lichtheim, *Ancient Egyptian Literature*, 196).

52. See 10:1 for this expression and the note.

53. In this verse, our poet mentions Yamm (the sea god) and Tannin (the dragon), both symbols of chaos. God must defeat chaos to order our world. Job is saying that he is not God's enemy; he is not going to return the world to chaos. Get real!

54. The object is missing in the text.

55. Here I correct the Hebrew text as in BHS.

The Rebel Job

¹⁷ What are human beings that you make them so great,
Or that you pay attention to them?
¹⁸ You have visited them every morning;
Every moment you test them.[56]
¹⁹ How long will you not turn your gaze from me?
Will you not let me alone till I swallow my spit?
²⁰ Have I sinned? What am I doing to you, O watcher of humanity?
Why have you made me your target?
Am I, myself, a burden?
²¹ Why don't you lift[57] my transgression,
And make my iniquity pass away?
For now, I shall lie down in dust,[58]
And you will search for me, but I shall not be there.[59]

8 ¹ **Bildad the Shuhite answered; he said**:
² How long will you utter these [things]?
The words of your mouth are a mighty wind.
³ Does El pervert justice?
Does Shaddai pervert [the] right?
⁴ If your children have sinned against him,
He has sent them into the power of their transgression.
⁵ If you will search for El,
And from Shaddai seek mercy,
⁶ If you are pure and upright,
Now he will rouse himself for you;
He will restore your righteous dwelling.
⁷ Your beginning will seem a small thing;
Your end will be very prosperous.[60]

---

56. This is a parody of Psalm 8. See the note for 7:1 for an explanation of the plural forms.

57. *Lift*. This is connected to the last word in v. 20. One could translate: "Why don't you unburden my transgression?"

58. *In dust*. Or in the netherworld?

59. This expression is also used in v. 8 of this same chapter.

60. In vv. 5–7, we have the standard orthodox belief. Just turn to God and all will be well. This is the same as we find in **The Ancient Folktale of Job (Job I)** in the prologue and the epilogue. In v. 8, Bildad does not claim that this position is new. Not at all. It is

8 So, ask an ancient generation,
   And consider what their fathers discovered.
9 For we are of yesterday and do not know;
   For our days on earth are a shadow.
10 Will they not teach you, tell you,
   And bring forth words from their minds?
11 Does papyrus grow without a marsh,[61]
   Or a reed thrive without water?[62]
12 While it is still green, not yet cut,
   Before any other grass, it will wither.
13 Such is the way of all who forget El,
   And [the] hope of [the] impious shall perish:
14 Whose confidence snaps,[63]
   Whose basis of trust is a spider's house.
15 He leans on his house, and it does not stand.
   He grasps it, but it will not stay up.
16 He is moist before Shamesh,[64]
   And over his garden, his root spreads out.
17 His roots are interwoven over a pile of rocks;
   A house of stones he visions.
18 If he is swallowed up from his place,
   It will deny him: "I have never seen you!"
19 Such are the joy[s] of his way,
   And from another clod, they will grow.[65]
20 So, El does not reject a perfect person,
   Nor take the hand of evildoers.

---

the wisdom of the ancient scribes. See Lambert, *Babylonian Wisdom Literature*, 10–20. However, this is the position that the rebel Job (**Job II**) is against in chapters 3–26.

61. See *The Story of Sinuhe*, B 122, "What would join a papyrus marsh with a mountain of stone (my translation)."

62. *Papyrus* and *reed*. The Hebrew words for these two plants are most likely borrowed from Egyptian. The word for "reed" also appears in Ugaritic.

63. This is a difficult line, and this is only a guess. Others change the text and attempt to make "snaps" parallel with "spider's house/web" in the next line. So they translate "gossamer."

64. *Shamesh*. This could be taken as a divine name or just a noun for "sun."

65. What will grow? More of these "joys" that are not joys at all.

21 He will yet fill your mouth with laughter,
And your lips with shouts of joy.
22 Your enemies will be dressed in shame,
And [the] tent of the wicked will be no more.

9 1 **Job answered; he said**:
2 Indeed I know that [the following] is so:
What human can be acquitted before El?[66]
3 If one wanted to file a lawsuit with him,
He could not answer him once in a thousand.[67]
4 [Of the] wise of mind and mighty in strength,
Who has provoked him? [Who] has remained healthy?
5 The one who overturns mountains,
And they do not know that in his anger he overturned them;[68]
6 The one who shakes [the] earth from its place,
And her pillars tremble;
7 The one who commands the sun, and it does not rise;
He seals up [the] stars.
8 Who stretched out [the] heavens by himself,
And who trod on the back of Yamm.[69]
9 Who made [the] Bear, Orion,
Pleiades, and the Chambers of Teman.[70]
10 Who does great deeds which cannot be understood,
And wonders without number.

---

66. The rebel Job knows the answer, and it is "not one."

67. Notice that this Job is not at this point eager to go to court.

68. Verses 5–13 describe the powerful creator/god before whom the human does not have a chance. Here the rebel Job already knows all about this creator. He does not have to be informed by God, as is the case of the ancient Job (see Job 38–41). As noted above, even if Job does not believe in such a God he is still forced to deal with him. After this description, the poet continues the thought of vv. 2–4 in vv. 14–24.

69. To move from chaos to cosmos, God must defeat Yamm or the sea. At Ugarit Baal had to defeat Yamm and here El must do the same. In this verse the heavens and the earth are formed by the defeat of Yamm.

70. For a discussion of these constellations see Pope, *Job*, 70–71. They are listed again in Job 38:31–32. The Hebrew words are usually correlated in this way. "Teman," which I have left as a proper name means "south wind."

The Many Voices of Job

11 So, he passes me by, and I do not see [him];
    He goes on, and I cannot perceive him.
12 Thus he despoils; who can stop him?
    Who can say to him, "What are you doing?"
13 Eloah will not turn back his anger;
    The helpers of Rahab were prostrated beneath him.[71]
14 Indeed, could I answer him,
    Could I choose my words against him?
15 Him, though I am innocent, I could not answer;
    I would be pleading for mercy from my judge.
16 If I summoned, [if] he answered me,
    I do not believe that he would hear my voice.[72]
17 He who would crush me with a storm,[73]
    He multiplies my wounds gratuitously.
18 He does not allow me to catch my breath,
    But he stuffs me with bitterness.
19 If for strength, a mighty one is here;
    If for judgment, who will summon me?[74]
20 If I am right, my mouth would condemn me;[75]
    [Though] I am innocent; he has [already] declared me crooked.
21 I am innocent;
    I do not know myself;
    I loathe my life.
22 She is one. Therefore I said,
    "He destroys [both] innocent and guilty.

71. Rahab is another sea monster and symbol of chaos. Some creation traditions show how God defeated Rahab (note Psalm 89:10 and Isaiah 51:9).

72. This powerful God does not know how to listen.

73. I think the translation "storm / whirlwind" is better here than the Targum's "hair" (AB and Tanakh). Also note that God does crush the ancient and patient Job with his voice in the storm (Job 38–41). Here the rebel Job is looking back on that ancient story.

74. I do not think anyone has the correct translation for this verse. In fact, I am not so sure about mine. However, if mine is correct, what does it mean? I think it means if we are talking about who can win in a power struggle then the answer is obvious. It is this powerful God. If we are talking about a judgment in a court case, then the answer to the rhetorical question ("who will summon me?") is also obvious. It is this same powerful God.

75. As in v. 2, there is no human who can be acquitted before this God.

23 If a scourge suddenly kills,
   He mocks [the] despair of the innocent.[76]
24 Earth has been placed in [the] hand of [the] wicked;[77]
   The faces of her judges he covers.[78]
   If not, then who is he?"[79]
25 My days have been swifter than a runner;
   They fled; they saw nothing good.
26 They have raced by like reed boats,
   Like an eagle dives on prey.
27 If I say, "I will forget my complaint;
   I will change my face, and I will look cheerful,"
28 I remain in fear of all my pain;
   I know that you will not acquit me.
29 I will be guilty.
   Why should I work in vain?
30 If I washed myself with soap,
   And I purified my palms with lye,
31 Then you would dip me in the pit [of slime],[80]
   And my clothes would abhor me.
32 For he is not a man, like me, whom I could answer,
   "Let us come together in the trial."
33 There is no arbiter between us
   To lay his hand on us both.
34 Let him turn away his club from me,
   Let his dread not terrify me,
35 [Then] I would speak, and I would not fear him.
   But I am not so with him.[81]

---

76. It would be difficult to say anything that would be worse about this God.

77. Note that it is not the righteous who will inherit the earth.

78. The rulers of this earth have been blinded by God. So, there is no justice; that is a basic theme in this poem (see Job 19:7 and 12:13).

79. Another rhetorical question. Of course, it is God who has done this.

80. Compare this with the opposite view in **Job I**, 30:23 and in Elihu's first speech in Job 33:18-30 and another similar view of the rebel in Job 17:13-14 below.

81. The MT has "with me." Here I follow the LXX. In any case, it is clear that the rebel Job was afraid to go to court with such a God.

The Many Voices of Job

10 ¹ My soul is disgusted with my life;
   I will give free rein to my complaint;
   I will speak from the bitterness of my soul.[82]
² I will say to Eloah, "Do not condemn me;
   Let me know for what you are charging me.
³ Does it seem good to you that you oppress,
   That you despise the labor of your hands,
   And on the counsel of [the] wicked you have beamed?
⁴ Do you have eyes of flesh?
   Or do you see as a human sees?
⁵ Are your days like [the] days of a human?
   Or are your years like [the] days of a hero?
⁶ That you seek out my iniquity,
   And you search for my sin.
⁷ You know that I am not guilty,
   And there is no one who can escape from your hand.
⁸ Your hands shaped me; they made me,
   [Then] a complete turnaround, you have destroyed me.
⁹ Remember that you formed me as clay;
   And you will return me to mud.[83]
¹⁰ Did you not pour me out as milk,
   And curdle me as cheese,
¹¹ Clothe me [with] skin and flesh,
   Knit me with bones and sinews?[84]
¹² Life and kindness you gave me;
   And your visitations guarded my being.

82. In my earlier translation I translated Hebrew *nephesh* as "being." Here and at the beginning of this verse, I have changed this to "soul." I have been influenced by my work with the Egyptian story: *A Dialogue between a Man and His Ba*. See Fisher, *Tales from Ancient Egypt*. Also note 7:11 above.

83. *Mud*. This could be translated with the traditional "dust," but it really refers to the "dirt, mud, or slime" of the netherworld. I have translated Genesis 3:19b, "For you are clay, / And to clay you shall return," using "clay" instead of the traditional "dust." In light of this passage in Job, I am tempted to translate, "For you are clay, / And to mud you shall return." Also see Job 4:19 above.

84. Verses 10 and 11 metaphorically deal with the conception and development of the human fetus within the womb, and v. 12 goes beyond that to suggest God's care of the infant.

13 These [things] you hid in your mind;
   I knew that this was your way.
14 If I sinned, you were watching me;
   From my iniquity, you would not clear me.
15 If I were guilty, woe is me;
   If I were innocent, I could not lift my head,
   Sated with shame and seeing my misery.
16 As a lion is bold, you stalk me;
   You return; you show yourself wondrous against me.
17 You renew your witnesses against me;
   You multiply your anger against me;
   [Always] changes, but hardship [remains] with me.[85]
18 Why did you bring me from the womb?[86]
   I would have expired;
   Not an eye would have seen me.
19 That which I was not, I would have been;
   From womb to tomb, I would have been carried.[87]
20 Are not my days few? Desist!
   Stand away from me, and let me smile a little
21 Before I go (and I will never return)
   To [the] netherworld of darkness, to the shadow of Mot,[88]
22 A netherworld of darkness like gloom,
   A shadow of Mot and chaos;
   [This netherworld] was as bright as gloom."[89]

11 1 Zophar the Naamathite answered; he said:
2 Should a multitude of words not be answered?
   Or should an articulate man be acquitted?

---

85. My translation of this difficult line is only a guess.
86. Here he goes back to the theme of chapter 3.
87. I follow Pope's translation, "Carried from womb to tomb" (*Job*, 73).
88. *Shadow of Mot.* See 3:5 for this same expression. Mot is the god of death. For the idea of "no return" note all of the passages listed in my note on 16:22.
89. The Hebrew reads, "She was brightened like/with gloom." I take it that "she" refers to "earth / netherworld." In any case, this is a terrific line to end this speech.

3 Should your idle talk silence men?
 When you have mocked should no one be humiliated?
4 You have said, "My doctrine is pure,
 And I am clean in your eyes."[90]
5 But would that Eloah might speak,
 Might open his lips against you.
6 He would tell you [the] secrets of wisdom,
 For there are two sides to sound wisdom.
 Know that Eloah forgets, for you, some of your iniquity.[91]
7 Can you discover the hidden nature of Eloah,
 Or can you discover the limits of Shaddai?
8 [The] heights of [the] heavens, what can you do?
 Deeper than Sheol, how can you know?
9 Longer than [the] earth is its measure
 And broader than Yamm.[92]
10 If he should pass on, or imprison,
 Or call an assembly, who can turn him back?[93]
11 For he has known worthless men;
 He has seen iniquity, and will he not understand?
12 An empty headed man will get understanding,
 When the wild ass of the steppe is born domesticated.[94]
13 If you had [only] redirected your mind,
 If you had spread out your palms to him,
14 If you have iniquity in your hand, remove it,
 And do not allow wrongdoing to dwell in your tents.
15 Then you will lift up your face without defect;
 You will be firm, and you will not fear.

---

90. *Your.* This refers to God's eyes. In other words, God knows that Job is "clean," but he punishes Job even so. This is unjust. Others translate, "You are clean in your own eyes" (Pope, *Job*, 83, and the note on 84).

91. Therefore, according to Zophar, God is more just than Job thinks he is.

92. *Yamm.* Either "Yamm," the god of the sea or "[the] sea."

93. This covers all situations. God can overlook a mistake or sin; he can punish, or he can call an assembly to judge someone. You cannot change this.

94. See Pope, *Job*, 86, and note Genesis 16:12.

16 For you will forget trouble,
   You will remember [it] as water that has flowed by.⁹⁵
17 Life will be brighter than noon;
   Darkness will be like morning.
18 You will trust, because there is hope;
   You will search for security [and] sleep well.
19 You will bed down, and no one will disturb.
   Many will seek your favor.
20 [The] eyes of [the] wicked will fail;
   A way of escape has been taken from them;
   Their hope is the last breath of life.⁹⁶

12 1 Job answered; he said:
2 Indeed, you are [educated] people,⁹⁷
   And with you wisdom will die.⁹⁸
3 But I have a mind even as you;
   I am not less than you.
   Who does not know such things as these?⁹⁹
4 A laughingstock to his friends, that is me.
   He who called to Eloah; he answered him;
   [He is] a perfect and righteous laughingstock.¹⁰⁰
5 For disaster is contemptuous in [the] thought of those at ease,
   Prepared for those whose feet slip.
6 The tents of the violent are at ease,
   And security belongs to those who enrage El,
   Whom Eloah carried in his hand.

95. Perhaps: "You will remember it as water under the bridge."
96. This last line of Zophar's speech tries to surpass the final line of Job's speech in 10:22.
97. Pope, *Job*, 88 refers to them as "gentry."
98. Verse 2 is sarcastic. The fact is that these so-called friends are not educated. They are indoctrinated, and wisdom will not die with them.
99. This question refers to the rest of this chapter that lists all such things. It does not refer back to what Zophar claims in chapter 11.
100. These three lines are difficult. I think the first line refers to Job, and the next two refer to his "friends." In other words, the one who calls on Eloah is also a laughingstock but a righteous one. Job in 9:16 has already stated that it is useless to call on God.

⁷ But indeed, ask please the domestic animals,
   And they will teach you;
   And the birds of the heavens, they will tell you.
⁸ Or speak to the earth,[101] she will teach you.
   And the fish of the sea will recount to you.
⁹ Who does not know among all of these,
   That the hand of Eloah[102] has done this?
¹⁰ [He] in whose hand are all living beings
   And the spirit of all human flesh.
¹¹ Does not [the] ear test words,
   And the palate tastes its food?
¹² Among [the] aged is there wisdom,
   Or is there understanding in length of days?
¹³ With him is wisdom and might;
   His are counsel and understanding.[103]
¹⁴ If he tears down, it cannot be rebuilt.
   He imprisons a person, and he cannot be set free.
¹⁵ If he withholds the waters, they dry up;
   If he lets them go, they devastate [the] earth.
¹⁶ With him are strength and insight;
   To him belong the deceived and the deceiver.
¹⁷ He makes counselors walk about disrobed,
   And judges he drives mad.
¹⁸ [The] belt of kings he has loosened;
   He bound a cloth on their loins.
¹⁹ He makes priests walk about disrobed,
   And the well established he overturns.
²⁰ He deprives [the] faithful of speech,
   And [the] judgment of elders he takes away.

101. This could be the netherworld.

102. The MT has "Yahweh," but this name for God is not used elsewhere in this poem. There are some Hebrew texts with "Eloah." I do not know which name to use, but I doubt if the rebel would use the name that is used so much in **Job I**. Since this verse is extremely sarcastic, I suppose the rebel could have used "Yahweh" in his anger against the "friends" and their God. The "friends" think they are so wise, but they are in fact so very mistaken. The other animals know that Eloah is responsible for the injustice in this world.

103. Again the point is that God is responsible for the injustice. See 19:7 and 9:24.

21 He has poured contempt on princes,
And has loosened [the] belt[s] of nobles.[104]
22 He has revealed [the] mysteries from darkness;
He has brought to the light the shadow of Mot.[105]
23 He has made the states great; he has destroyed them.
He has scattered the states; he has led[106] them [away].
24 He has deprived the minds of the leaders of the people of the earth;
He has made them wander in chaos [with] no path.
25 They grope in darkness with no light;
He has made them stagger like the drunk.

13 1 There, my eye has seen everything;
My ear has heard; it has understood.
2 I, even I, know that which you know;
I am not less than you.[107]
3 Indeed, I want to speak to Shaddai;
I will be pleased to argue with El.[108]
4 And indeed, you are the ones who cover up lies;
You all are worthless healers.
5 Who will insure that you are totally silent?[109]
If [someone could], that would be wisdom for you.

104. Verses 18–21 are a unit. Verses 18a and 21b make the same point in order to begin and conclude this unit. In the court procedures, as known from the texts of Nuzi, there was an ordeal of belt wrestling. If you could remove the belt of your opponent, you were declared innocent. God declares himself innocent even though he does these evil things. Pope discusses this in commenting on Job 38:3a (*Job*, 291, but even though he credits C. H. Gordon with this observation, he tends to not take it seriously by showing the objections of H. L. Ginsberg and by not making a decision on the matter. Gordon has discussed this in many places; Pope (*Job*, 291) cites Gordon, "Belt Wrestling in the Ancient World."

105. *Shadow of Mot.* Here God can do away with Mot's shadow or "protection." Therefore, God is wise, powerful, and in control of Mot (the god of death, see 3:5; 10:21b; and Psalm 23:4), but he is still responsible for evil.

106. We are told in our grammars that this "leading" never has a negative sense, but the reason that we can come up with such "rules" is that we obey the rules in order to prove them.

107. This line is the same as 12:3b.

108. Here Job feels very bold. One wonders if he means it in light of chapters 9 and 10? In those chapters he knows that he would not stand a chance before God.

109. *Who will insure?* This is from "who will grant?" and is usually taken as an expres-

6 Hear, now, my argument,
   And attend the accusations of my lips.[110]
7 Is it for El that you speak unjustly?
   And for him will you speak deceitfully?
8 Will you declare El's innocence?[111]
   Or for El will you plead?[112]
9 Will it be well when he examines you?
   Or as one deceives a person, can you deceive him?
10 He will surely rebuke you,
   If in secret you declare [him] innocent.[113]
11 Will not his fear terrify you,
   And his dread fall upon you?
12 Your arguments are slimy[114] proverbs;
   Your defenses are defenses of clay.
13 Be silent before me, and I will speak.
   Let come upon me whatever.[115]
14 I will take my flesh in my teeth,
   And my soul I will place in my palm.[116]
15 So, he will kill me; I have no hope.
   Yet, I will argue my case to his face.[117]

---

sion of a wish (see 11:6). Pope translates, "I wish you would keep strictly silent" (*Job*, 96). This is the way it is translated by most, but at this point I would really rather keep the literal form and pose the question (though this forces the addition in the next line).

110. The imperatives in this verse are directed at those who are to remain silent. "Accusations" is a legal term, and the term is used again in v. 8b.

111. Literally, "Will you lift up his face?"

112. *Plead*. Once again a legal term.

113. This implies that such a God is not ashamed of what he does be it good or evil.

114. *Slimy*. This word is usually translated as "dust." Once again it is parallel with clay, and it can also mean "slime."

115. Another warning as in v. 5 to remain silent.

116. Whatever these sayings mean, I think they follow up on v. 13. Job will take responsibility for what comes from his actions. "My soul" here should be compared to 10:1 and 7:11.

117. This was one of the best-known verses in the KJV. Verse 15a read: "Though he slay me, yet will I trust him." Of course it was completely mistranslated and made a statement about the ancient Job (See the Inroduction).

16 Also, he could be my salvation,
    For no impious one would come to his face.[118]
17 Listen closely to my words,
    And my declaration be in your ears.
18 There, now, I have arranged a just case.
    I know that I am innocent.
19 Who is he who will contend with me?
    For then I would keep silent and expire.
20 O El,[119] do only two things for me,
    Then from your face I will not hide.
21 Remove your palm from me,
    And let your dread not fall upon me.
22 Summon me and I will answer,
    Or let me speak, and you reply to me.
23 How many are my iniquities and sins?
    Make known to me my transgression and my sin.
24 Why do you hide your face,
    And count me as your enemy?[120]
25 Will you terrify a driven leaf,
    Or will you pursue dried up chaff?
26 For you write bitter things against me,
    And you cause me to inherit the iniquities of my youth.
27 You put my feet in the stocks,
    And you watch all my ways;
    You put your mark on the soles of my feet.
28 He wastes away like a rotten thing,
    Like a moth-eaten garment,

14 1 A human, born of woman,
    Is of few days and sated with strife.

118. This renewed hope is only for a wavering moment. It cannot be sustained.

119. *El.* I read "El" instead of a negative particle with the same consonants. For this reading also see Habel, *The Book of Job*, 225. The negative just does not work. In vv. 20–27, Job is addressing God.

120. *Enemy.* Here we have a real pun. One could translate, "And count me as your Job / enemy." "Job" and "enemy" are both written with the same basic consonants (in "Job" the "y" is doubled) but with different vowels: Job = ʿ*iyyov* and enemy = ʿ*oyev*.

2 Like a flower that came forth; he withered;
   Like a shadow, he fled, and he does not endure.
3 Indeed, on such a one you opened your eye;
   And me, you bring into judgment with you.[121]
4 Who can produce [the] clean from [the] unclean?
   Not One![122]
5 If his days are determined,
   The number of his months with you,
   You have set his limits, and he cannot exceed.
6 Turn from upon him, and he may rest,
   Until he enjoys, as a hireling, his day.[123]
7 Yes, there is hope for the tree;
   If it is cut down, it will grow again,
   And its young shoots will not cease.
8 Or, if its root grows old in the earth,
   And in the dirt its stump dies,
9 At the scent of water, it will sprout,
   And make branches like a plant.
10 When a hero dies, he has collapsed;
   A human has expired, and where is he?[124]
11 Waters from the sea have disappeared.
   And a river dries up and is parched,
12 And a mortal has lain down, and he does not rise.
   They wake not until there are no heavens,
   And they rouse not from their sleep.

121. The human is too insignificant for God to bother with such a one.

122. This verse is difficult and may be an insertion. "*One*" refers to God; he cannot do the impossible. He is not all powerful! In the Ancient Mediterranean World the gods had numerical names. In Mesopotamia Anu is "One" and Adad is "Ten." In Egypt Amon-Re is "One," but see Cyrus H. Gordon, "His Name is One," where Gordon translates Zechariah 14:9 "on that day Yahweh will be one, and his name 'One.'" Also see Job 23:13 and 31:15.

123. This may not be much enjoyment, but anything is better than having God always watching.

124. *Where is he?* The answer to this question is well known; it is: "He is dead." In the Ugaritic texts when Baal dies, the same question was asked. "Where is Aliyan Baal? / Where is the Prince, Lord of the Earth?" (UT 49:IV: 29, 40). "Where is the prince?" is the meaning of the name Jezebel.

13 O that you would hide me in Sheol,
   Conceal me until your anger passes,
   Set for me a time, and remember me.
14 If a hero dies, will he live again?
   All the days of my service, I will endure,
   Until my relief comes.
15 You would call and I, I would answer,
   For the work of your hands, you would long.
16 But now you number my steps;
   You should not watch over my sins.
17 My transgression would be sealed in a parcel;
   You would plaster over my iniquity.
18 But if a mountain falls, it collapses,
   And a rock moves from its place.
19 Water has worn away stones,[125]
   Its torrents wash away earth's soil,
   And you have destroyed man's hope.
20 You overpower him forever; he has gone.
   You change his face; you have dismissed him.
21 His children receive honor, and he does not know,
   And they become insignificant, and he does not perceive them.
22 Only his own flesh pains him;
   His own soul mourns him.

15 1 **Eliphaz the Temanite answered; he said**:
   2 Does a wise one answer windy knowledge,
      And does he fill his belly with an east wind?
   3 Should he argue with speech that is not profitable,
      And words in which there is no value?
   4 Indeed you destroy religion,[126]
      And you do away with meditation before El.
   5 For your iniquity instructs your mouth,
      And you choose a crafty tongue.

---

125. I use the past tense in a line like this, because that is what we are dealing with. Other translations use the present here and elsewhere. They seem to think it is easier.

126. *Religion.* This is a translation of the word "fear."

⁶ Your mouth condemns you, not I,
  And your lips testify against you.
⁷ Were you [the] first human[127] born,
  And were you brought forth before the hills?
⁸ Do you listen in the council of Eloah,
  And do you limit wisdom to yourself?
⁹ What do you know that we do not know?
  [What] do you understand that is not with us?
¹⁰ Even gray headed and aged are with us,
  Older in days than your father.[128]
¹¹ Are the consolations of El too little for you,
  And a gentle word with you?
¹² What takes from you your mind,
  And why are your eyes failing,
¹³ That you turn your wind against El;
  You throw out a word from your mouth?
¹⁴ What is man that he can be pure,
  And that he can be righteous, one born of woman?
¹⁵ Even his holy ones, he distrusts,
  And the heavens are not pure in his eyes.
¹⁶ How then one who is abhorred and foul,
  Man who drinks iniquity like water?
¹⁷ I will tell you, listen to me,[129]
  And what I have seen, I will declare,
¹⁸ What sages make known,
  And their fathers did not conceal,
¹⁹ To whom alone the land was given,
  And no alien passed among them.[130]

127. *Human.* Here the Hebrew is ʾ*adam*, as in Genesis 1–4, but without "the"; and, of course, note Job 14:1 and 10.

128. Job has already questioned (Job 12:12) those who equate the elderly with the wise.

129. In vv. 17–35, Eliphaz gives his orthodox view that the wicked will suffer for their deeds.

130. In other words what follows comes from the sages and their fathers and was not borrowed from any outsider. Again this is not true, but you cannot expect the truth from Mr. Orthodox or Eliphaz.

The Rebel Job

20 [The] wicked writhes in pain all his days,
 And few years have been stored up for the ruthless.
21 Dreadful sounds are in his ears;
 When all is well, the enemy falls upon him.
22 He does not believe in returning from darkness,
 And he is destined for the sword.
23 He wanders for food; where is it?[131]
 He has known that fixed in his hand is a day of darkness.
24 Distress and anguish terrifies him,
 [Anguish][132] overpowers him
 Like a king ready for attack,
25 Because he lifted his hand against El,
 And against Shaddai he acts as a hero.
26 He charges at him with neck chains,
 With the thick bosses of his shields,
27 For he has covered his face with his fat;
 He has gained great muscle on [his] loins.
28 He has dwelt in ruined cities,
 [In] houses, no one lives in them,
 Which are ready for heaps of rubble.
29 He will not be rich, nor will his wealth endure,
 Nor [his] possessions reach the netherworld.
30 He will not escape from darkness,
 A flame will wither his shoot,
 And he will depart from the breath of his mouth.[133]
31 He should not trust in vanity, being misled;
 For vanity will be his reward.
32 Before his time is complete,
 His branch did not grow green.
33 He will ruin, like a vine, his unripe grapes;
 And he will cast, like an olive tree, his blossom.

---

131. At 14:10 we discussed this question, "Where is he?" Here the question is about the same, and the answer is "There is none."

132. I supply "anguish" (a fem. noun) instead of the "she" contained in the verbal form.

133. Or to turn it around, his breath will depart from him.

The Many Voices of Job

> ³⁴ For an irreligious band is desolate,
>   And fire devours tents of bribery;
> ³⁵ Pregnant with pain and giving birth to evil,
>   Their womb has produced deceit.

16 ¹ **Job answered; he said:**
> ² I have heard many things like these;
>   Painful comforters are you all.
> ³ Is there a limit to windy words?
>   Or what afflicts you that you[134] answer?
> ⁴ I too could speak like you,
>   If you were in my place.[135]
>   I could string words together against you,
>   And I could shake my head at you.
> ⁵ [Or][136] I could strengthen you with my mouth;
>   The quivering of my lips would bring relief.
> ⁶ If I speak, my pain will not be relieved;
>   And if I desist, what departs from me?
> ⁷ But now he[137] has exhausted me;
>   You have destroyed my entire community.
> ⁸ You have compressed me;
>   It has become a witness.
>   My leanness has risen against me;
>   It testifies to my face.
> ⁹ His anger has torn and assaulted me;
>   He has gnashed his teeth against me.
>   My enemy narrows his eyes at me.

134. Some object to the singular "you" at this point, but I think the poet can turn to one of the so-called comforters and ask such a question.

135. This is a common and good translation, but it does stand at some distance from the Hebrew, which reads: "If there were [to me] your being instead of my being."

136. I have inserted "or" at this point, because it seems that there are two options if Job were in their place: 1) he could be nasty or 2) he could bring some comfort. Pope is concerned about such an abrupt transition between vv. 2–5 and v. 6 and following, but v. 5 is the transition (*Job*, 123). Verse 6 does go back to Job's suffering. It is a nice touch to use the word "relief" in both vv. 5b and 6a.

137. This is God. After he makes this statement, Job in turn slides into the second person.

10 They have opened wide their mouths against me;
    They have slapped my cheeks with scorn;
    Together they mass themselves against me.
11 El hands me over to [the] vicious,
    And into the hands of the wicked he throws me.
12 I was at ease; he shattered me,
    And he grabbed me by the neck; he broke me in pieces.
    He set me up as his target.
13 His archers surround me;
    He splits my kidneys; he shows no compassion;
    He pours out my gall on the earth.
14 He slices me, slice upon slice;
    He rushes against me like a warrior.
15 I have sewed sackcloth over my skin,
    And I have thrust my horn in dirt.[138]
16 My face is reddened with weeping;
    Upon my eyes is the shadow of Mot,[139]
17 Although there is no violence on my palms,
    And my prayer is pure.[140]
18 O earth, cover not my blood,
    And let there be no tomb[141] for my outcry.
19 Even now, my witness is in the heavens;
    And my witness is in the heights.
20 My interpreters, my friends,
    To Eloah my eyes have cried,
21 And let him plead for a hero with Eloah,
    [Like] a human[142] for his friend.

138. He has given up all his power and his glory. "Slime" could be translated as "dirt," or "mud," but the traditional dust does not work among all of the blood, gall, and guts.

139. Most translate "darkness." Job is near death.

140. Usually the rebel Job is not interested in prayer, but it is understandable that the person who is suffering can go back and forth on such an issue. He does not think God hears the prayers of the suffering; at times he thinks this God is dead. But, when things get really bad, and one is near death, it is natural to want to cry out.

141. *Tomb.* Here the Hebrew means, "place," but this word is also used for a sanctuary or any place where rituals are held, such as a tomb.

142. The Hebrew behind "human" is "Ben-Adam" or "Son of Adam."

The Many Voices of Job

²² For a number of years will come,
And the way of no return, I will go.[143]

17 ¹ My spirit is broken;
My days are finished;
[The] tombs are for me.
² Surely, the mounds are before me,
And in their slimy pits, my eye fixes its gaze.
³ Make a pledge for me with you!
Who is he who will strike my hand?[144]
⁴ Since you have closed their mind from reason,
Therefore you must not exalt them.
⁵ He [who] informs on his friends for a reward,
The eyes of his children will fail.
⁶ He has made me a byword of the peoples,
And I exist for spitting in my face.
⁷ My eye was dimmed because of anguish,
And my body parts were all like a shadow.
⁸ [The] upright are astonished at this,
And [the] innocent are aroused against the impious,
⁹ And [the] righteous holds to his way,
And [the] clean-handed grows in strength.
¹⁰ But all of you return and come now,
And I will not find a wise one among you![145]
¹¹ My days have passed,
My plans have been broken,
My mind's possessions.
¹² They make night into day;
Light is near to the face of darkness.
¹³ If I wait for Sheol [as] my home,
In the dark I have covered my bed,

---

143. Once again this reminds one of *The Harper's Song* in Egypt (Lichtheim, *Ancient Egyptian Literature*, 196). "The way of no return" has been a constant theme (3:14; 4:20; 7:10; 10:21; and now in 16:22).

144. We could say, "Who will shake my hand."

145. In vv. 8–10 Job is mocking his so-called righteous friends; they may be righteous, but they are archconservatives. They hold to their ways, but they are not wise. This is pure sarcasm (Good, *In Turns of Tempest*, 251).

The Rebel Job

14 To the pit I have called forth, "You are my father,"
   To the maggot, "My mother and my sister,"
15 Then where, where is my hope?[146]
   My hope, who can see it?
16 It will descend into the power of Sheol;
   We shall rest in the slime together.

18 1 **Bildad the Shuhite answered; he said:**
2 How long will you[147] set snares of words?
   You should [all] be sensible, and afterward we could speak.
3 Why are we considered as domestic animals?
   Deemed dull in your eyes?
4 One who tears himself in his anger,
   Will earth be abandoned on your account,
   [Or] a rock be moved from its place?[148]
5 Indeed, [the] light of the wicked is extinguished,
   And the flame of his fire does not shine.
6 [The] light in his tent became dark,
   And his lamp above him is extinguished.
7 His strong strides are shortened,
   And his own plan throws him down.
8 For he has been thrown by his feet into the net,
   And he walks on a pit-fall.
9 A trap seizes [his] heel;
   A snare lays hold on him.
10 His noose is hid on the earth,
    And his trap is on [the] path.[149]

146. Once more we have the "where" question (see note at 14:10). The answer as before is: it's gone; it's dead; there is no hope. Following the "where question" is "who can see it." Since these two questions are related, chapter 23 is the right place for Job's "where is God?" It is here that he cannot be found. In vv. 11–16 Job is certain of his death and his burial in Sheol (the place of the dead). In burial rituals, the living can be blessed and have hope if they "call forth" (*qara'*) the names of their fathers or mothers. Here Job has no hope, and he can only "call forth" to the "pit" and the "maggot."

147. *You.* This is in the plural. Bildad groups Job with all sinners.

148. Job's anger will not change the world or the doctrine of retribution, that is, the rock, which is described again in the following two verses.

149. There are several lines from v. 7 through v. 10 that are not easy to explain, but in

61

The Many Voices of Job

11 On all sides terrors have fallen upon him;
   They drive him to his feet.
12 Let his strength be famished,[150]
   And calamity is ready at his side.
13 He[151] devours his skin with two hands,
   The first-born of Mot[152] with both his hands.
14 He is torn form his tent, his security,
   And he is marched to the King of Terrors.[153]
15 In his tent is set fire;
   On his abode is scattered brimstone.
16 From below his roots dry up,
   And from above his branch withers.
17 Memory of him has perished from [the] earth,
   And he has no name upon the face of the land.[154]
18 He shall drive him from light into darkness,
   And he[155] shall chase him from [this] world.
19 He has no offspring and no posterity among his people,
   And there is no survivor in his old haunts.[156]

---

general it is clear that the wicked will be caught. This is Bildad's view.

150. It is tempting to follow Pope ("The Ravenous One confronts him, . . .") who follows Dahood (Pope, *Job*, 135), but I cannot delete the verb "to be" at the beginning of the line.

151. This "he" is "the first-born of Mot" (the god of death) as spelled out in the next line.

152. Here I follow Pope (*Job*, 135), who goes along with Sarna. Now I think if the "first-born of Mot" is some kind of a royal title, it should also be compared to Ugaritic *rb tmtt*, "Chief of Death" or "Master of Death" (*PRU* V, 81). On this, Gordon says that the title means "Lord of Killing" (*UT*, 431). I think in all this we are dealing with some "Executioner" or our "Grim Reaper."

153. Once again, I follow Pope who depends on Moran (*Job*, 136). The "King of Terrors" equals Mot.

154. *Upon the face of the land*. For this same expression see Job 5:10.

155. This "he" and that of the first line is obtained by reading the consonantal text which is vocalized to give plural subjects to these lines. I take it that the "he" refers to Eloah or Mot.

156. In Psalm 37:28 and 29, there is this same view. The wicked will have no survivors. The lack of progeny is the concern in many stories. Note the Ugaritic *Epic of Aqhat and Danel* and Epic of Keret. In Isaiah 14:20, we see the real impact of such thought. The dead need proper burial, and they need someone to call forth their names in the tomb rituals.

The Rebel Job

20 On his [last] day, westerners were appalled,
And Easterners were seized with horror.
21 Surely these were the dwellings of [the] wicked,
And this is [the] place of one who did not know El.

19 1 Job answered; he said:
2 How long will you torment me
And crush me with words?
3 You humiliate me; this is ten times.[157]
You are not ashamed; you abuse me.
4 And even if, truly, I have erred,[158]
My error remains with me.
5 Though, truly, you are overbearing against me,
And you argue my disgrace against me.
6 Know then that Eloah has perverted me,[159]
And he has thrown his net over me.
7 So, I cry, "Violence," and I am not answered;
I cry for help, and there is no justice.[160]
8 He has blocked my way, and I cannot pass;
He has set darkness upon my paths.
9 He has stripped my honor from me;
He has removed the crown from my head.
10 He breaks me completely down; I am gone.
He has uprooted my hope like a tree.
11 He has kindled his anger against me;
He considers me as one of his foes.
12 His troops come in together;
They have built seigeworks against me;
They camped around my tent.
13 He has sent my confederates far from me,
And he has estranged my friends from me.

---

157. The "friends" have made five speeches thus far, but they have humiliated Job at least ten times.

158. Here Job does not admit anything.

159. Hence, God as in Job 8:3 in fact perverts justice, and in v. 7, there is no justice.

160. *There is no justice*: a major theme of the rebel. See 9:24 and 12:13.

14 My relatives and intimates have gone;
The guests of my house have forgotten me,[161]

15 And my maids consider me as a stranger;
I have become a foreigner in their eyes.

16 I summoned my slave, but he does not respond.
With my mouth I implore him.

17 My breath was offensive to my wife,
And I was loathsome to my own children.[162]

18 Even urchins despised me;
If I would rise up, they spoke against me.

19 All the men of my association[163] have abhorred me,
And those whom I have loved have turned against me.

20 My bones have stuck through my skin and my flesh;
I, myself, have escaped by the skin of my teeth.

21 Have pity on me; have pity on me, O you my friends,
For the hand of Eloah has struck me.

22 Why do you pursue me like El?
Are you not satisfied with my flesh?

23 O that my words would be written,
Would be engraved on the stela,[164]

---

161. This line is made up of the last word of v. 14 and the first two words of v. 15.

162. This line has always been a problem to all interpreters, because in the ancient story, Job's children have all died. So, these children have been understood as grandchildren, uterine brothers, and in many other ways. However the rebel Job does not follow the ancient Job in most of his thoughts or actions. If the rebel Job also lost all his children, what sense does this make? It makes no sense the way most translators ignore the tense factor in this verse (also in other verses). However, since this is in the past tense, Job could have been "loathsome" to his children even before they were killed. But we really do not know anything about the rebel Job's children.

163. *The men of my association*. This association or club/lodge should be compared to the Ugaritic *mt mrzh*, "Man/men of the Marzeah." This was an association for cultic celebrations and banquets, and they also were engaged in mourning rites for the dead (see Jeremiah 16:5–9). For a study of the Marzeah text from Ugarit see Fisher, *The Claremont Ras Shamra Texts*, 37–54.

164. Perhaps this is "the stela" at his tomb. The rebel Job was not as fortunate as the Harper whom we have mentioned several times above (Lichtheim, *Ancient Egyptian Litersture*, 194–97) in connection with death being final. The Harper's song from the tomb of King Intef is the most interesting. This song or at least a copy of it was engraved on the wall of a tomb; this is remarkable to engrave such skepticism in the land where immortality was the rule. Note the refrain in vii, 2: "Make holiday, / Do not weary of it! / Lo,

24 With an iron stylus and lead.[165]
   They would be carved in rock as a witness.[166]
25 But as for me, I know that my avenger[167] lives;
   And a guarantor[168] by [my] grave[169] will stand.[170]
26 This, even after my skin has been peeled off,
   And without my flesh, shall I see Eloah?[171]
27 Whom shall I see who is for me?
   My eyes saw no stranger.[172]
   My heart[173] is destroyed in my bosom.
28 Because you say, "How will we pursue him?"
   (And [the] root of the matter is found in me.)
29 Fear for yourselves before the edge of the sword,
   For these things are crimes [deserving the] sword,
   So that you may know Shaddayan.[174]

20 1 **Zophar the Naamathite answered; he said**:
   2 Surely, my disquieting thoughts cause me to answer,
     And because of my inner turmoil,

---

none is allowed to take his goods with him, / Lo, none who departs comes back again!"

165. It seems that the incised letters in the rock were filled with lead.

166. Here I follow Pope's suggestion in his notes (*Job*, 145) where he relates this to Isaiah 30:8. The rebel Job's words were not incised in stone, and in fact they were buried or wrapped in the ancient story of Job.

167. *Avenger*. This is a kinsman who will be an avenger of blood (2 Samuel 14:11) or look after interests of his kinsman.

168. *Guarantor*. So Pope, *Job*, 139 and 146. Even if this word is translated in the usual "And that at last" the avenger is still at the grave as a witness.

169. *Grave*. The Hebrew word means in this context "dust/slime" rather than the netherworld.

170. Here the avenger will stand to testify on behalf of Job.

171. I cannot prove that this is a question, but I think it is, and the answer is, "No!" The context demands this sense.

172. Rather he saw his avenger.

173. *Heart*. The Hebrew word is actually "kidney," but in English "heart" works better as the seat of one's emotions.

174. *Shaddayan*. This is a form of Shaddai, a divine name that we have seen before. In vv. 28 and 29, the rebel Job is throwing the orthodoxy of his "friends" back in their faces. As sinners they will have to face judgment.

3 I listen to the rebuke that [creates] my shame,
   So the spirit of my understanding replies to me.
4 Have you not known this from old,
   Since a human was placed on earth,
5 That [the] triumph of [the] wicked is brief,
   And [the] joy of [the] impious is for a moment?
6 If his pride reaches up to the heavens,
   And his head touches the clouds,
7 He will perish forever like his own dung;
   They who saw him will say, "Where is he?"[175]
8 Like a dream he will fly away, and they will not find him,
   And he will flee like a vision of [the] night.
9 An eye that saw him will do so no more;
   His place will not see him again.
10 His children will seek the favor of [the] poor,
   And his hands return his wealth.
11 His skeleton was full of his youthfulness,
   And with him it will lie down in the slime.
12 When evil is sweet in his mouth,
   He hides it under his tongue,
13 He savors it, and he will not let it go,
   And he retains it under his palate;
14 His food in his guts has been changed;
   The venom of vipers is within him.
15 Wealth he swallowed; he disgorged it.
   El expels it from his belly.
16 [The] venom of asps he shall suck;
   [The] tongue of a viper shall slay him.
17 He shall see no streams:
   Rivers [and] wadies of honey and yogurt.
18 He is the one who shall return his gain not consumed,
   That is, the wealth of his trading, and he shall not rejoice.
19 Because he has crushed [and] forsook [the] poor,
   [And] he has seized a house that he did not build,

---

175. *Where is he?* Once again we have this question, and everyone knows the answer. He is dead. Also see the notes for 14:10; 17:15; and 23:9.

The Rebel Job

20 Because he has not known ease in his belly,
    In his greed, he does not allow [any] to escape.
21 There is nothing left for his meal,
    Therefore his good times will not endure.
22 In the fullness of his plenty, he shall know distress;
    Every powerful misery will come upon him.
23 He shall have his belly filled.
    He[176] shall send on him his burning anger,
    And it shall rain down into his bowels.
24 He will flee from an iron weapon;
    A bronze bow will pierce him.
25 He pulled; it came out from his[177] back,
    Lightning[178] from his gall.
    Terrors come upon him.
26 Complete darkness awaits his treasured ones,
    An unfanned fire will consume him.
    Who survives in his tent will be injured.
27 [The] heavens shall reveal his iniquity,
    And the earth will rise up against him.
28 A flood[179] shall roll away his house,
    Torrents on the day of his wrath.
29 This is [the] lot of a wicked human from Elohim,
    And [the] inheritance appointed him from El.

21 1 **Job answered; he said**:
    2 Listen closely to my words,
        And let this be your consolation.
    3 Bear with me, and I will speak,
        And after my speech, mock on.

---

176. This "he" equals God.

177. I have moved the conjunction before "lightning" to the preceding word ("back") and used it for "his."

178. Others translate "lightning" as a "gleaming point or sword."

179. Here I follow Pope once again (*Job*, 153).

4 Am I for humans [in] my complaint?[180]
   And if so, why should I not be impatient?
5 Look at me and be appalled,
   And lay [your] hand upon [your] mouth.
6 Whenever I have remembered, I have been terrified;
   My flesh is seized with shuddering.
7 Why do the wicked live on?
   They have grown old;
   They have even become wealthy.
8 Their seed has been established in their presence with them
   And their offspring before their eyes.
9 Their houses are safe from fear,
   And the rod of Eloah is not upon them.
10 His bull has bred and never fails;
   His cow calves and never aborts.
11 They send out their young ones as a flock,
   And their children dance about.
12 They take up the timbrel and harp,
   And they rejoice at [the] sound of [the] flute.[181]
13 They finish their days with good times,
   And in a moment they go down to Sheol.
14 They said to El, "Depart from us;
   The knowledge of your ways, we have not desired.
15 What is Shaddai that we should serve him,
   And what do we profit when we encounter him?"
16 So, is not their well-being in their hand?
   [The] counsel of [the] wicked is far from me.[182]
17 How often is [the] lamp of [the] wicked put out,
   Or does their calamity come upon them,
   Or does he[183] apportion pain in his anger?

180. The expected answer is "yes!"

181. *Flute*. The Hebrew word behind this translation is some kind of a musical instrument. "Flute" is a good guess.

182. Verse 16 is not difficult to translate, but it is difficult to understand how it relates to its context. Also note 22:18b.

183. This refers to God.

18 Are they as stubble before the wind,
   And as chaff [the] storm wind carried away?
19 [You say,] "Eloah stores up punishment for his children;"[184]
   He should pay him[185] that he might know.
20 Let his eyes see his destruction,
   And let him drink the wrath of Shaddai.
21 For what does he care about his house after him,
   When the number of his months has been cut off?
22 Does he teach knowledge to El,
   Does he judge [the] highest?
23 One dies with perfect bones,
   Wholly at ease and tranquil.
24 His vessels are full of milk,
   And the marrow of his bones is moist.
25 And another dies a bitter person,
   And he never tasted the good [life].
26 They lie together on the slime,
   And worm[s] cover them.
27 Look, I have known your plans
   And devices you are plotting against me.
28 For you say, "Where is the royal house,
   And where are [the][186] dwellings of [the] wicked?"
29 Have you not asked those who travel [the] road[s],
   And do you not acknowledge their evidence,
30 That on the day of disaster [the] wicked is spared,
   From the day of fury they are led forth?
31 Who will tell [him] to his face his way?
   And who will pay him [for what] he has done?[187]
32 So he is carried to the graves,
   And upon [the] mound [one] guards.

184. This is an old view that Job thinks is unjust. See Exodus 34:7.

185. That is, any one of his children.

186. Here I have left out the word "tent" which may have functioned as a determinative.

187. The answer is "no one." Certainly not God, because there is no justice and probably there is no God (at least not this kind of God).

33 [The] clods of [the] wadi were sweet to him,
And after him all humans will follow,
And before him [they are] innumerable.[188]
34 So how can you comfort me with air?
And your answers have remained fraudulent.

22 1 **Eliphaz the Temanite answered; he said:**
2 Can a man be of service to El,
Or a sage benefit him?
3 Is Shaddai pleased if you are righteous,
Or does he gain if you are perfect in your conduct?
4 Is it because of your piety he reproves you,
Enters into judgment with you?
5 Is not your wickedness great,
And your iniquities have no end?
6 Because you have taken a pledge from your brother unjustly,
And the clothing of the naked you have stripped.
7 You do not give the weary water to drink,
You withhold food from the hungry.
8 So a strong man owns the land,
And as one forgiven he dwells in it.[189]
9 Widows you sent away empty,
And the arms of orphans are broken.[190]
10 Therefore snares surround you,
And sudden dread frightens you.
11 Or darkness you will not see,
And a flood of waters covers you.
12 Is not Eloah [in the] height of [the] heavens?
And see [the] top of stars, for they have [always] been high.

---

188. In vv. 32–33 the evil one receives a great funeral. This should be compared to Isaiah 14:4–21 where the king of Babylon is the evil one, and he shall not have a great funeral. In fact he shall not be remembered or "called forth" in a funeral ritual. See my discussion of this in *Genesis: A Royal Epic*, 29.

189. The "strong man" who lives in it is probably Job. He is being accused of only caring for himself.

190. In this world any just person had to care for the widow and the orphan.

The Rebel Job

13 You say, "What does El know?
    Can he judge through the dark cloud?
14 Clouds hide him, and he does not see,
    And he walks around [the] circle of [the] heavens."
15 Do you watch the perpetual path
    That worthless men have walked,
16 Who were snatched before [their] time,
    A river washed away their foundation?
17 The ones who said to El, "Depart from us,[191]
    What can Shaddai do for us?"
18 Yet he filled their houses [with] good!
    So [the] counsel of [the] wicked is far from me.[192]
19 [The] righteous see, and they rejoice,
    And [the] innocent deride them:
20 "Surely their substance was destroyed,
    And a fire consumed their surplus."[193]
21 Serve[194] him and be complete;
    In this, good will come to you.
22 Take instruction from his mouth,
    And put his words in you mind.
23 If you return to Shaddai you will be restored;
    You shall put iniquity far from your tent.
24 So, set on the mud [your] gold,
    And on the rocks of the stream [your] Ophir.[195]
25 Shaddai will be your gold
    And a mountain of silver for you.
26 When you delight in Shaddai,
    And lift up your face to Eloah,
27 You shall pray to him, and he will hear you,
    And you shall fulfill your vows.

---

191. Compare 21:14a.

192. This is the same as 21:16b.

193. The first line of this verse is very difficult. In any case it is a bit of wishful thinking.

194. *Serve* is from *skn*. It is used in the same way in Ugaritic, UT 51:I: 21.

195. *Ophir* is the name of a land, which produced gold.

28 And you will decide something, and it will stand,
   And on your path, light has shone.
29 When some sank down, you said, "pride,"
   For [the] humble, he will save.
30 He will deliver the guilty,
   Who will be delivered by your clean hands.[196]

23 1 **Job answered; he said:**
2 Even today my complaint is bitter,
   [His] hand is heavy on account of my sighing.[197]
3 O that I knew where to find him,
   That I might come to his dwelling.
4 I would set [my] case before him,
   And I would fill my mouth with arguments.
5 I would [like] to know [the] words he would answer me,
   And I would understand what he would say to me.
6 Through an attorney would he prosecute me?
   Surely not! He would charge me.
7 There [the] upright could reason with him;
   I could bring forth my case to an enduring life.[198]
8 Lo, I go east, and he is not there,
   And west, and I cannot discern him.
9 North, in his work place, and I do not behold [him].
   He hides in the south, and I do not see [him].[199]

---

196. With this Eliphaz covers all his bases. The not-so-innocent can be helped by the innocent. This is not what Eliphaz usually says, but it is what happened in the ancient story of Job where the three friends were not innocent and Job helps to cleanse them. See Job 42:7 and 8.

197. The more Job suffers, sighs, and groans, the more this God increases Job's heavy burden.

198. This was certainly not the way that Job thought about his case in chapters 9 and 13. This must be completely sarcastic; it is tragic irony. We need Job's tone of voice in vv. 5-7. In any case, the situation just alluded to in vv. 5-7 will never be according to vv. 8-9.

199. In 23:3 plus 8-9, Job cannot find God. He is really saying, "Where is he?" From 14: 7-12 we found out that to ask this question means that God is dead. This is the way a much later person, Elihu, whom we meet in Job 32-37, understood Job 23:8-9. Note Elihu's words in Job 35:9-10 (see the note on these verses in chapter 4, "The Speeches

10 But he knew [the] way to me;
   He tested me;²⁰⁰ I will emerge as gold.
11 My foot stays in his path;
   His way I have kept, and I will not stray.
12 I will not depart from the command of his lips;
   In my bosom I have treasured the words of his mouth.
13 But he is One;²⁰¹ who can change him?
   And his being has desired [something]; he has done it.
14 So, he will execute my sentence,
   And many such things are with him.
15 Therefore I am dismayed before him;
   I consider, and I am afraid of him.
16 El weakened my heart,
   And Shaddai has terrified me.
17 For surely, I am annihilated by [the] faces of darkness,
   And my face covered by dark gloom.²⁰²

24 1 Why are [the] times not treasured by Shaddai,
   And [why] do those who know him not perceive his days?²⁰³

---

of Elihu"), "From great oppression, they cry; / They cry out for help from the arm of the mighty, / But none has said, 'Where is Eloah, my maker, / Who gives strength in the night, / Who teaches us more than the beasts of the earth, / And makes us wiser than the birds of the heavens?'" God is dead (at the least absent), but as we go on through this chapter and the next, it is clear that Job still fears, at least at times, this do-nothing God who cares for no one and does not even exist. Or is it that when Job still believed in this God, he did walk the straight and narrow, and it was all for nothing?

200. If **The Rebel Job** ever contained a prologue, there was probably no "adversary" or "*hasatan*," but rather God himself did the testing (as with Abraham, Genesis 22). This may also be the case in an early form of **The Ancient Folktale of Job**. See chapters 1 and 2.

201. See Job 14:4 and the note on "One." Also see Job 31:15

202. Job can declare that the God of his friends is not to be found. He is dead. But that same God is so much a part of Job's culture, if not his religion, that in the dark of night the faces, the presence, and the gloom still produce terrors of the night.

203. This is a difficult verse. Why should Shaddai be concerned about the times? If he is dead, absent, or immortal, time does not matter. However it does for mortals and for those who suffer. No one really knows about God's actions or his days. I do not know what all of this means, but this much is clear: this God does not care.

2 They[204] remove boundaries;
   They have stolen flocks; they have pastured [them].
3 They drive away [the] donkey of [the] orphan;
   They take the widow's ox for a pledge.
4 They push the needy from [the] road;
   [The] poor of [the] land hide themselves together.
5 Like wild asses in the steppe,
   They go out to their work,
   Seeking hopefully for food;
   Surely, [the] desert [yields] food for the young.
6 They harvest fodder in the field,
   And they glean [the] vineyard of [the] wicked.
7 Naked they pass the night without clothing,
   And they have no covering from the cold.
8 They are wet from [the] mountain rain,
   And without shelter, they stay close to [the] rocks.
9 They snatch the orphan from the breast,
   And they take the suckling of the poor as security.[205]
10 Naked they go without clothing,[206]
   And hungry, they carry [the] sheaves.
11 Between their rows they press oil;
   They have stomped [the] wine-vats;
   They were thirsty.
12 From [the] city [the] dying groan,
   And a person with wounds cries out.
   Yet Eloah does not pay attention to prayer.
13 They, yes, they have been among those who rebel [against the] light;
   They have never known its ways,
   And they have never dwelt in its paths.[207]

204. Many substitute "the wicked" for "they."

205. In 24:2–4 there is a description of the wicked, and in 5–8 the description is of the poor. Here in v. 9, we seem to repeat this dual description, but this time the wicked only get one verse. Or does v. 9 belong with 2–4?

206. This line begins as does v. 7, and we are back to a description of the poor.

207. From here to the end of this chapter, it is difficult to know what is going on, because there are not enough clear transitions. It is difficult to know who is speaking and to whom. The RSV added at the beginning of v. 18 "You say" and thus Job is quoting his

14 At daylight [the] murderer arises;
   He kills [the] poor and [the] needy,
   And in the night he becomes like the thief.
15 [The] eye of the adulterer watches for twilight,
   Saying, "No eye will see me,"
   And he puts a cover over [his] face.
16 In the dark such a one has dug into houses;[208]
   By day they shut themselves up;
   They do not know [the] light.
17 Yes, it is the same for them, morning and deep darkness,[209]
   Yes, they are acquainted with the terrors of the shadow of Mot.
18 "Swift is he on the surface of the water;[210]
   Cursed is their portion in the earth,
   He does not turn on [the] way to [the] vineyards.[211]
19 Drought and heat steal [the] water of [the] snow,
   [As does] Sheol those who have sinned.
20 [The] womb forgets him;
   His sweetness is [the] worm;
   He is remembered no more;
   Injustice has been broken like a tree."

---

opposition and their ideas. At this point others have removed 18–25, and they put it in a hypothetical final speech of Zophar after Job 27:8–23 (see Pope, *Job*, 188–89). I will leave it in its present place with the following understanding: 1) vv. 13–17 is another description of the wicked by Job. 2) vv. 18–20 is indeed Job quoting or mocking his opponents. 3) vv. 21–23a seems to be an additional accusation by Job. 4) vv. 23b–24 is once again Job quoting (with a snarl) what his opponents are sure to say. 5) v. 25 is Job's final challenge, and there is none, who can answer him.

208. They dig under the walls of a house.

209. *Deep darkness*. I have usually translated this as "the shadow of Mot / death" as I do in the next line. At the beginning of this line I have "Yes" instead of "For." This is what I have done in Genesis 4:23–24 where I followed the "Ja" of Buber and Rosenzweig in their translation, *Die Fünf Bücher der Weisung*.

210. As I said above, I think Job is now quoting or mocking his opponents. They believe that such evildoers will be punished. This section is 18–20.

211. Who is he? Some say God, but I do not know. The main point is that the evildoers will not do well.

The Many Voices of Job

21 He is the one, who feeds on the barren woman with no child,
And he does no good for [the] widow.[212]

22 He[213] has prolonged [the life of the] mighty with his power.
He[214] arises but cannot believe in life.

23 He[215] gives him security,
And he is sustained.
"But his eyes are on their ways.

24 They were exalted for a moment, but it is gone.
And like the head of grain, they wither."[216]

25 If it is not so,[217] who will prove me a liar,
And make as nothing my words?

25 1 **Bildad the Shuhite answered; he said**:[218]

2 Dominion and dread are with him;[219]
He is the one who makes well being in his heights.

3 Is there a number to his troops,
And upon whom does his light not rise?

4 How can a man be righteous before El,
And how can one born of woman be pure?

5 Even [the] moon does not shine,
And [the] stars have not been pure in his eyes.

---

212. Job in this new accusation says "no" to the quotation in vv 18–20. Injustice is not broken; the barren and the widow are still oppressed by the mighty ("he" = the oppressor in this verse).

213. This is God.

214. This is the oppressor.

215. This is God.

216. This was the opponents' stock answer, but it does not impress Job. He wants them to prove him wrong as we note in the next verse.

217. That is, the opponents' answer in 23b–24.

218. Many scholars add some material to this answer of Bildad. They say that it is too short. Pope adds 26:5–14 (*Job*, 180–81). However, I do not think this is necessary. All of chapter 26 belongs to the final word of the rebel Job. Bildad's last speech is short, and Zophar does not come up with a final speech. I sometimes feel sorry for these two. For me Eliphaz is their leader, and an example of how a smart leader with a conservative bent can lead astray.

219. This "him" is God.

6 How much less a man, a worm.
  And the son of Adam, a maggot.

26¹ Job answered; he said:[220]

2 How have you helped [the] powerless?
  Have you aided a weak arm?
3 How have you counseled [the] unwise,
  Or made known wisdom to a multitude?
4 With whom have you uttered words,
  Whose breath came forth from you?[221]
5 The Raphaim[222] writhe
  Under the waters and their inhabitants.
6 Naked is Sheol before him,[223]
  And Abaddon[224] has no covering.
7 He is the one who stretched out Zaphon[225] over chaos;
  He is the one who suspended the earth on nothing.[226]
8 He is the one, who bound the waters in his clouds,
  And a cloud does not break because of them.
9 He is the one who obscured [the] face of [the] full moon;
  He spread over it his cloud.
10 He made a circle on the surface of [the] waters
  As a boundary of light with darkness.

---

220. 26:1-4 is put just after 27:1 by Pope (*Job*, 187). I disagree with this, because as I see it chapter 27 belongs to **The Ancient Folktale of Job**. Job 27:1 continues the scene in 2:9-13. The story of the rebel Job is only found in chapters 3-26. For this I can only imagine a prologue and an epilogue, but the story is a negative response to **The Ancient Folktale of Job (Job I)**.

221. So these words did not come from God.

222. The Raphaim are the inhabitants of the netherworld, who are summoned during rituals for the dead.

223. "Him" = God

224. *Abaddon*. This means, "to perish," and is another term for the netherworld.

225. *Zaphon*. In the Ugaritic texts this is the sacred mountain of Baal where he builds his temple (a replica of the earth) from which he can rule the world. In Psalm 48 Mount Zion is located, mythologically speaking, on Zaphon. Here God orders the world from chaos (as in Genesis).

226. Does this speak of the earth as in space?

11 [The] pillars of [the] heavens tremble,
   And they are astounded from his rebuke.
12 By his power he stilled the Sea;
   By his cunning he smashed Rahab.[227]
13 By his wind the heavens were cleared;
   [By] his hand he pierced the fleeing Serpent.
14 Lo, these are just traces of his rule;
   What a whisper of a word we hear from him;[228]
   Who can understand the thunder of his might?

---

227. To have power over the Sea and Rahab means that you can bring order out of chaos.

228. We do not know much about God; this was important to the rebel Job. He does not believe in the God of his opponents even though at night he sometimes still fears him. He will go so far as to say that their God does not exist. But even if one needs to talk about another God who has power over chaos and can order the world, what does that mean? Very little. Why? Because, "What a whisper of a word we hear from him," and "who can understand the thunder of his might?"

Where Can Wisdom Be Found?
Job 28

3

INTRODUCTION

The poet of Job 28 has given us a beautiful hymn, which in its final form seems to agree with the point of view expressed in **Job I**. After all, it is clear that the ancient Job is a God-fearing man, and now in v. 28—a later addition to Job 28—an editor says that this also makes him wise. This hymn was inserted in **Job I** at some later date after the editor added v. 28. The hymn is a marvelous poem concerning mining, and the author shows a real awareness of geological formations and activities. But Job 28 also says that humans cannot find wisdom, and when this later editor added v. 28, he reversed the main point of the hymn. Reversing its position entirely, v. 28 says that wisdom belongs to the one who fears God.

Job 28 makes it clear that wisdom is beyond value, that wisdom cannot be purchased, and that wisdom's endurance will surpass rubies. Humans are not able to find wisdom. The rebel Job would probably value the poem more than the words of his three opponents, who are always pretending to be wise as they try to defend the ways of the ancient Job and his orthodoxy. In fact, if this hymn were in its original form, the rebel Job could have used it in his debate. But after some pious editor added v. 28, the hymn was radically changed, and now it could be used in the narrative of the ancient Job.

The Many Voices of Job

WHERE CAN WISDOM BE FOUND?

1. Yes, there is a smelter[1] for silver,
   And a place where they refine gold.
2. Iron is taken from ore,[2]
   And stone produces copper.
3. [Man] made an end to darkness,[3]
   And to every end he searches
   [For] dark and gloomy rock.
4. Foreign people[4] broke shafts,
   [Shafts] forgotten by pathways,
   They hung; [far] from men they swayed.[5]
5. Earth, food comes from her,
   And under her, it was changed by fire.[6]
6. Her stones are [the] source of sapphire,
   And particles of gold are in them.
7. [The] path no raptor has known,
   And [the] falcon's eye has not seen it.
8. [The] proud beasts have not used it;
   [The] lion has not come upon it.[7]
9. [Man] put his hand into the flint;
   He overturned mountains from [the] root.
10. In the rocks he hewed out channels,
    And his eye saw every precious thing.
11. [The] sources of the rivers he stopped,
    And hidden things he brought to light.

---

1. Most translators translate "mine," but "smelter" seems better as a parallel to the next line.

2. Some translate "dust."

3. These ancient miners used lamps.

4. The foreign people were used in the mines.

5. Perhaps these pathways were like rope bridges.

6. This is a fantastic line. It refers to the heat that is instrumental in creating metamorphic rock where we find gemstones.

7. In vv. 7–8 we are probably dealing with tunnels of which the birds and beasts know nothing.

Where Can Wisdom Be Found?

12 And wisdom, where can she be found?
   And where is [the] place of understanding?
13 Man does not know her dwelling,
   And she cannot be found in the land of the living.
14 Tehom[8] said, "She is not with me,"
   And Yamm[9] said, "Not with me."
15 Fine gold cannot be given for her,
   And silver cannot be weighed out [as] her price.
16 She cannot be purchased with the gold of Ophir,
   With precious onyx or sapphire.
17 Gold and glass cannot equal her,
   Nor vessels of fine gold be her exchange.
18 Coral or crystal will not be mentioned;
   [The] endurance of wisdom surpasses rubies.
19 The topaz of Ethiopia cannot equal her;
   She cannot be purchased with pure gold.
20 And wisdom, from where does she come?
   And where is [the] place of understanding?
21 She is concealed from [the] eyes of all living;[10]
   From the birds of the heavens she is hidden.
22 Abbadon and Death said,
   "With our ears we have heard a rumor of her."
23 Elohim has understood her way,
   And he has known her place.
24 For he looks to the ends of the earth;
   He sees everything under the heavens:
25 Giving weight to the wind
   He measured the waters with a measure.
26 When he made a channel for the rain
   And a path for the thundershower,
27 Then he saw her, and he evaluated her;
   He established her, and he tested her.

---

8. This word for "The Deep" is related to the Babylonian goddess Tiamat.
9. The god Yamm can also be translated "The Sea."
10. A human does not have a chance of finding Wisdom.

28 He said to the human,[11]
"See, the fear of Adonai,[12] that is wisdom,
And to turn from evil is understanding."

THE FEAR OF THE LORD

In my novel, *The Minority Report*, Keziah and her husband Jonathan live on the campus of The Jerusalem Academy with their family. Jonathan is one of the scribes and teachers at the academy, and Keziah is the author of *The Minority Report*. She and Jonathan have many minority opinions. In this novel Jonathan is the author of **The Rebel Job** and Keziah writes and discusses other minority opinions such as "The Fear of the Lord," and I want to share some of her thoughts after she read, "Where Can Wisdom Be Found?" The following is a summary of her thoughts:

Among the majority of the scribes, the fear of God, the Lord, or Yahweh is the beginning of wisdom or can be equated with wisdom. The ancient Job is described as "one who feared Elohim and avoided evil." This majority view is not difficult to hold. After all when David took Bathsheba and had her husband, Uriah, killed, the prophet Nathan said that God would kill their child.[13] Also in the story of Judah, Yahweh killed Judah's first two sons.[14] If Yahweh is like that, he is a God to fear. Likewise the God in *The Ancient Story of Job* is to be feared. On this last point Jonathan has found a recently edited poem by one who is a loyal follower of the ancient Job.

Since Jonathan has created a poem, **The Rebel Job**, which was written to crush **The Ancient Folktale of Job**, he is interested in what this new poet has written and how a recent editor has changed it and thereby remaining faithful to the ancient Job. The editor's point of view is not

---

11. "To the human" is from the Hebrew *la'adam*. As in Genesis 2, *'Adam* is not a proper name. "Humankind" works well here.

12. *'Adonai* is usually translated as "Lord." This is the only place in the Book of Job where Adonai is used. Some pietistic editor added this last verse to the hymn before inserting it into this narrative of the ancient Job. In doing so he completely changed or reversed the intent of the hymn. We were told all along that humans cannot find wisdom, and suddenly in v. 28, wisdom belongs to one who fears God.

13. Second Samuel 12:15.

14. Genesis 38.

Where Can Wisdom Be Found?

good, but the original poetry is actually a masterpiece. Jonathan calls this poem, "Where Can Wisdom Be Found?" This poem makes wisdom so remote and unobtainable that a mere human does not have a chance of finding it. Certainly, human skill in mining is not true wisdom, and of course wisdom cannot be purchased. It is only God who knows wisdom. This is great, and the three "friends" of my rebel should read this. But this editor contradicts the entire poem when he adds, "He said to the human, / 'See, the fear of Adonai, that is wisdom, / And to turn from evil is understanding.'"[15]

Keziah's father was Gad, and she says that my father, Jonathan and I have always had a different opinion concerning the nature of God than we find in this poem. Actually we do not know much about him. Perhaps he ordered this not-so-perfect world and made life possible for us, but there is no need to fear such a God and to do so hardly would seem to be the beginning of wisdom. For us wisdom is born of understanding based on observation. Note one of our favorite accounts of the birth of a proverb:[16]

> I passed by the field of a lazy man,
> And by the vineyard of a senseless man.
> Here, thorns climbed up all over them.
> Its surface was covered with weeds,
> And its stone wall was broken down.
> I observed; I took it to heart.
> I saw; I studied [this] lesson:
> A few naps, a few drowsy times,
> A few times of folding the hands to rest,
> And your poverty will come marching on,
> Even as a [charging] warrior your dire straits.

Here the sage has learned something about "poverty" or "dire straits." The lazy farmer will have nothing. But the important thing to note is the method of the sage. The sage observes and studies. We suggest that the conclusion is exaggerated, because the sages also talk about the need to

---

15. Job 28:28.
16. Proverbs 24:30–34.

enjoy one's work and to rest (this is true for all of us, the humans and the other animals as well). In fact we have another proverb that says:[17]

> The fool is one who folds his hands
> And the one who devours his flesh.
> Better is one handful of rest
> Than two handfuls of labor and [the] pursuit of wind.

Our view is that wisdom is the result of observation and study. It does not come from the fear of the Lord.

---

17. Ecclesiastes 4:5–6.

The Speeches of Elihu

4

INTRODUCTION

These speeches are attributed to Elihu,[1] but they are based on old arguments of those who challenged the author of **The Rebel Job** (Job 3–26). Thus they represent the *majority opinion* of state and altar, which was organized against the *minority opinions* in **The Rebel Job**. These speeches are unfair, unreliable, dull, and a senseless commentary on **The Rebel Job**, but they help us to understand the nature of the opposition to the rebel Job, and in some instances we are given a better understanding of the rebel based on the rage he provoked.[2] They should have been inserted just after 3–26, because in their present location these speeches interrupt the story line of **The Ancient Folktale of Job** or **Job I**.

JOB 32–37

32 ¹These three men[3] ceased answering Job, because from his viewpoint, he was right. ²The anger of Elihu, son

---

1. Is he the brother of David?
2. Elihu accuses Job of rebellion. See my note for 34:37.
3. Verses 1–5 give us an editorial transition relating 32–37 to 3–26 or Job II. In 3–26 "these three men" are called "friends," who are really the rebel's opponents, but here in the transition they are called "men" in vv. 1 and 5. However the editor or narrator refers to Elihu and his "friends" in verse 3, and they are in fact his opponents; his anger burned against them as well as Job. These are the "friends" in the dialogue and not the "friends""of Job I with the same names, though Elihu would not have liked them either. Yahweh faulted them in the Epilogue. It is obvious that 32–37 was inserted and interrupted the narrative flow of **Job I**.

of Barachel the Buzite of the clan of Ram, burned against Job; his anger burned, because [Job] made himself more right than Elohim. ³And against his three friends his anger burned, because they did not find an answer, yet they pronounced Job guilty. ⁴So Elihu waited for Job with words for [these men] were older than he. ⁵Elihu saw that there was no answer in the mouth of the three men; his anger burned.

> ⁶ **Elihu, son of Barachel the Buzite, answered; he said:**
> I am young in days, and you are old.
> Therefore I feared; I was afraid
> To make known my knowledge to you.
> ⁷ I said, "Days should speak,
> And many years ought to make known wisdom."
> ⁸ But it is [the] spirit in man,
> And the breath of Shaddai that gives understanding.[4]
> ⁹ [The] great ones do not give wisdom,
> Nor do [the] elderly understand justice.
> ¹⁰ Therefore I said, "Listen to me.
> I will make known my knowledge, even I."
> ¹¹ Here I have waited for your responses,
> So that I could weigh your understandings,
> Until you could search [for] words,
> ¹² And until I could understand you.
> But it was clear; Job did not have a judge;
> Not one of you could answer his words.
> ¹³ You cannot say, "We have found wisdom."
> El will defeat him, not man,[5]
> ¹⁴ And he did not arrange words against me,
> And with your words I will not refute him.[6]
> ¹⁵ They have been broken; they cannot answer again.
> Words have fled from them.

---

4. This is almost identical with the next chapter, 33:4. See my note there. Here he is saying that his friends are not inspired. But of course in 33:4 he is.

5. This viewpoint is like that of Job 28. He uses it against the three "friends."

6. Elihu constantly belittles the rebel's three opponents here and in the next two verses.

The Speeches of Elihu

16 And I waited, because they did not speak,
   For they stood; they did not answer again.
17 I will answer, even I, my portion;
   I will make known my knowledge, even I.
18 For I am full of words.
   The wind in my belly pushed me.
19 Therefore my belly is like unopened wine,
   Like new [wine] skins it will break.
20 I will speak, and it will break wind from me.[7]
   I will open my lips, and I will answer.
21 Please note: I will not forgive a man,
   And to a human I will not give a title.
22 For I do not know how I could give a title;[8]
   My maker would quickly carry me off."

ELIHU'S FIRST SPEECH

33 1 **So now, Job,[9] hear my utterances,**
   And give ear to every one of my words.
2 Please note, I have opened my mouth;
   My tongue has spoken from my palate.
3 My words are [from] an upright heart,
   And my lips have spoken pure knowledge.
4 The spirit of El made me,
   And the breath of Shaddai gives me life.[10]
5 If you are able, answer me.
   Prepare! Take your position before me.
6 See, I am like El's vessel;
   I, too, was nipped from clay.[11]

---

7. Elihu has to vent his anger.
8. Elihu will not give title or importance to his friends who could not answer Job.
9. This Job is obviously the rebel Job and not the patient Job of the ancient story. In Job 3–26 the three "friends" do not address the rebel by name.
10. Elihu claims to be inspired by God. Here he tries to outflank the rebel Job, who said that this was not the case with his three opponents. See Job 26:4.
11. Elihu claims to be inspired, but here there is a bit of false humility. I am just hu-

7 So, my terror should not frighten you,
   Nor should my pressure on you be heavy.
8 Indeed, you have said in my ears,
   And [the] sound of [the] words I hear,
9 "I am pure without transgression;
   I am clean and without guilt.[12]
10 Yet, he finds reasons to oppose me;
    He considers me his enemy.
11 He puts my feet in stocks;
    He watches all my ways."
12 On this, you are not right; I will answer you,
    For Eloah is greater than man.
13 Why have you accused him,
    [Is it] that he does not fulfill any of his words?
14 For El speaks in one [way],
    And in two, [yet] no one perceives it.
15 In a dream, a vision of the night,
    When deep sleep falls upon men,
    In slumbers upon [the] bed,
16 Then he uncovers [the] ear of men,
    And he seals their discipline
17 To turn a human [from] work,
    And pride from a hero he covers up.
18 He holds back his being from [the] Pit
    And his life from crossing the Channel. [13]
19 He is chastened by pain upon his bed
    And the strife of his bones is constant;

---

man and mortal.

12. The rebel Job did not make such claims.

13. This is similar to a passage in **The Ancient Folktale of Job**, 30:23: "But I know you will rescue me [from] Mot (or death)." In vv. 18–30 in this chapter the "Pit" is mentioned five times. It is another term for the abode of the dead or Sheol. Also the word "channel" is interesting. Marvin Pope says, "The Channel is the infernal stream, the river Hubur of Mesopotamian mythology and the Styx of the Greeks." Also note the completely opposite view concerning the "pit" in **The Rebel Job**: "Then you would dip me in the pit [of slime]," (Job 9:31a). Or also note Job 17:13-14, where the rebel has no hope.

The Speeches of Elihu

20 His life makes food loathsome to him,
And his being [loathes] fine meals.

21 His flesh disappears from view;
His bones, [which] were not seen, appear.

22 His being drew near the Pit
And his life to [the] Angels of Death.

23 If there is by him an angel,
An interpreter, one from a thousand,
To declare to a human his right,

24 Who favored him; who said:
"Deliver him from going down into the Pit;
I have found a ransom."

25 Healthier is his flesh than a boy's;
He returns to the days of his youth.

26 He prays to Eloah; he accepted him.
He saw his face with joy.
He returned to [the] man his righteousness.

27 He sings before men; he said:
"I sinned, and I perverted the right,
And he did not pay me back.

28 He saved my being from passing into the Pit,
And my life sees the light."

29 So, all these things El does,
Twice, three times with a man,

30 To turn back his being from [the] Pit,[14]
To light [him] with the light of life.

31 Heed, Job; listen to me.
Be silent, and I will speak.

32 If there are words, answer me;
Speak, for I have desired your righteousness.

---

14. This emphasis on the "Pit" is the same as we find in the Babylonian parallels to **The Ancient Folktale of Job**. The Babylonian text is *Ludlul bêl nêmeqi, or I Will Praise the Lord of Wisdom* (Lambert, *Babylonian Wisdom Literature*, 59) and look at IV, lines 5, "He rescued me [from the pit]," and 35, "Marduk can restore to life from the grave." Elihu would have made a great Babylonian sage.

33 If you have nothing, listen to me;
Keep silent! I will teach you wisdom.

ELIHU'S SECOND SPEECH

34:1 Elihu answered; he said:
2 Hear, O wise ones, my words,
And those who have knowledge, give ear to me.
3 For the ear tests words,
As [the] palate tastes food.
4 Justice we will choose for ourselves;
We will know among us what is good.
5 For Job has said, "I am righteous,[15]
And El has taken away my justice.
6 Concerning my justice will I lie?
I am wounded [by] my arrow [though] sinless."
7 What man is like Job?
He drinks mockery like water,
8 He wanders with ones who do evil
And goes with wicked men.
9 For he said, "A man gains nothing,
From his favor with Elohim."
10 Therefore, men of understanding, hear me.
Far be it from El to do evil,
And from Shaddai to do wrong.
11 He will pay a human for work,
And as to [the] path of man, he causes him to find it.
12 Surely El would not cause evil,
And Shaddai would not pervert justice.

---

15. See Good, *In Turns of Tempest*, 142, who says that Elihu is again misquoting Job. Good translates "innocent" instead of my "righteous." That is allowed, but the main point is that "I am innocent" in 9:15 and 10:15 is preceded by "if." The rebel does not make such claims. Pope points to 27:2 for such a claim, but this is not the rebel Job speaking (Pope, *Job*, 256), but rather the ancient Job.

The Speeches of Elihu

13 Who appointed him over [the] earth,
And who ordered [the] entire world?
14 If he sets his mind to it,
He can take back his spirit and his breath.
15 All flesh would expire together,
And humankind would return to slime.[16]
16 If [you] have understanding, hear this;
Give ear to the sound of my words.
17 Can one who hates justice restrain [you]?
Or will you condemn [the] great Righteous One?
18 Is it him who calls a king scoundrel,
[Or] nobles wicked,[17]
19 Who has not forgiven princes,
Nor favored [the] rich over the poor?
They are all the work of his hands.
20 [In] a moment they die, and [in the] middle of the night;
People are shaken and pass away;
[The] mighty are removed without a hand.
21 For his eyes are on a man's conduct,
And he sees all his steps.
22 There is no darkness, no shadow of Mot,
Where evildoers can hide.
23 For he does not set a time for man
To go to El in judgment.
24 He shatters the mighty without a search,
And he sets others in their place.
25 Therefore he knows their deeds;
He overturns night, and they are crushed.
26 With [the] wicked he struck them down
In a public place.

16. Apparently Elihu has not read the story of Noah and the flood or perhaps he does not believe Elohim's promise in Genesis 9:11 ("never again shall all flesh be cut off by the waters of the flood"). But perhaps he is not talking about the flood. He goes back to God's forming the human in Genesis 2:5–7. He would have God undo this work by taking back the "breath of life," and all flesh would expire. His God is not nice.

17. Elihu and the orthodox want the religious who fear God to also be obedient to the state.

27 Because they turned away from following him,
   And they did not heed any of his ways
28 To bring before him [the] cry of the poor,
   And he might hear [the] cry of the afflicted.[18]
29 If he is silent, who can condemn?
   If he hide his face, who can see him,
   Other than a group or an individual alike?
30 From [the] reign of an impious human,
   [There is] more than snares for [the] people.
31 For has he said to El, "I have asked forgiveness,
   I will not act corruptly;
32 What I cannot see you teach me;
   If I have done evil, I will not do [it] again?"
33 Shall he repay it from what you have
   Since you despise [him]?
   So you choose and not I,
   And whatever you know, speak.
34 Intelligent men will say to me,
   And a wise man who hears me:
35 "Job speaks without knowledge,
   And his words are unintelligible.
36 Job ought to be tried until the end
   On account of answers from evil men.
37 For he adds to his sin rebellion;[19]
   He strikes out among us,
   And he multiplies his words against El."

---

18. It seems that Elihu is trying to speak against the rebel's words in 24:12: "From [the] city [the] dying groan, / and a person with wounds cries out. / And yet Eloah does not pay attention to prayer."

19. The Hebrew behind "rebellion" is usually translated as "transgression," but in the verbal forms it means, "to rebel" or "to transgress." In the nominal forms it is usually "transgression," but this should not always be the case. The NRSV translates "rebellion." This makes sense. It would be strange to say, "He adds to his sin transgression." No, he adds "rebellion." It is Elihu who calls the Job of 3–26 a rebel.

The Speeches of Elihu

ELIHU'S THIRD SPEECH

35¹ **Elihu answered; he said:**
² Do you consider this justice?
Do you say, "My righteousness is greater than El's"?
³ That you say, "What does it profit you,
What do I gain from my sin?"
⁴ I will answer you [with] words,
And your friends[20] with you.
⁵ Look to the heavens and see,
And behold [the] clouds; they are higher than you.
⁶ If you have sinned, what are you doing against him?
If your transgressions have multiplied, what are you doing to him?
⁷ If you have become righteous, what are you giving to him?
Or what does he take from your hand?
⁸ Your wickedness belongs to a man like yourself
And your righteousness to a human being.
⁹ From great oppression they cry out;
They call for help from the arm of the mighty.
¹⁰ And nobody has said, "Where is Eloah my Maker?[21]
Who gives strength in the night,
¹¹ Who teaches us by the beasts of the earth,
[And] he makes us wise by the birds of the heavens." [22]

---

20. Who are these friends? Perhaps these are the rebel's opponents, and Elihu would like to teach them as well.

21. This may be one of the most important lines in the speeches of Elihu. In chapter 2, "The Rebel Job," I have written extensive notes for Job 23 and have quoted this question in line 10a. Elihu is saying that many have suffered, but they have not asked this question. But he implies that the rebel Job asked it. I think Elihu was correct on this point. In **The Rebel Job** we cannot find the line where the rebel asks, "Where Is God?" Some editor could have removed such a line, but we will never know. But we do not need to find such a line or even imagine it, because the rebel searches for God and cannot find God. This is in Job 23 and the rebel surely said to himself, if to no other, "Where is he?" I have shown in my comments for **The Rebel Job** that the answer to this question is always the same: "he is dead." Elihu is convinced that since Job cannot see God (v. 14a), he has asked the question that Elihu's oppressed people would never ask.

22. Compare this to Job 12:7–8

The Many Voices of Job

12 There they cry out, but he does not answer
  Before [the] pride of [the] evil men.
13 Surely, El does not listen to deceit,
  And Shaddai does not look at it.
14 Indeed you say [that] you cannot see him.
  [The] case is before him; you should wait for him.
15 And now, there is nothing that his anger has punished,
  And he has not known much folly.
16 And Job? In vain he opens his mouth;
  He multiplies words without knowledge.

ELIHU'S FOURTH SPEECH

36 1 Elihu continued; he said:
2 Wait for me a little, and I will show you
  That for Eloah there are still [more] words.
3 I will bring my knowledge from afar,
  And I will grant righteousness to my maker.
4 For truly my words are not false;
  Perfect knowledge is with you.
5 So, El is mighty, and he does not hate;
  [He] is mighty [and] strong of heart.[23]
6 He will not let the wicked live;
  And justice he gives to [the] oppressed.
7 He does not withdraw his eyes from the righteous,
  And with kings on the throne,
  He has enthroned them forever;
  They have been exalted.[24]
8 And when they are bound in fetters,
  [Or] should they be caught in cords of distress,

---

23. The rebel Job says that God is not all-powerful.

24. Verses 6 and 7, if compared to the rebel Job's words, make exactly the opposite point. That Elihu is a pro-monarchy scribe is clear: kings are enthroned forever. This would seem to place Elihu after the time of Solomon when "enthroned forever" was royal propaganda (Psalm 89:27–37).

The Speeches of Elihu

9 He has always told them what they have done,
  And their transgressions that they magnify.
10 He has opened their ear to discipline;
   He has said that they should turn from evil.
11 If they listen and serve [him],
   They will end their days in the good,
   And their years with the pleasures [of life].[25]
12 And if they do not listen, they cross the Channel, [26]
   And they expire without knowledge.
13 [The] impious of heart display anger;
   They do not cry out when he has chastised them.
14 Their soul dies when young
   And their life among the male prostitutes.
15 He rescues [the] afflicted by his affliction,
   And he opens their ear by the oppression.
16 Indeed, he has lured you from [the] mouth of distress,
   [To] a broad expanse instead
   And the comfort of your table full of rich food.
17 But you are full of judgment of [the] wicked;
   Judgment and justice will be upheld.
18 But beware, lest he allure you by riches,
   And let not a great bribe mislead you.
19 Will he compare your cry when there is no distress
   With all your powers of strength?
20 Do not long for the night,
   [When] people go up [from] their place.
21 Take care, do not turn to evil,
   For with this you were proven through affliction.
22 Lo, El is exalted in his power;
   Who is a teacher like him?
23 Who has reproached him [for] his conduct?
   Or who has said, "You have done wrong?"

---

25. To this the rebel Job would come up with a resounding, "No." "To listen" means "to obey."

26. Compare this use of "Channel" to 33:18b above.

24 Remember to extol his work,
   Of which men have sung.
25 Every human has seen it;
   Mankind sees [it] from afar.
26 Lo, El is great,
   And we do not know the number of his years,
   And [they] cannot be counted.
27 When he draws up drops of water,
   They form rain for his flood,
28 Which [the] clouds trickle down;
   They pour on the ground showers.
29 Can anyone understand [the] spreading of a cloud,
   The thundering [from] his booth?
30 Lo, he spread his lightning over it,
   And he covered the roots of the sea.
31 For with these things he judges peoples;
   He gives food in abundance.
32 Lightning covered [his] palms;
   He commanded it to attack.
33 His thunder speaks concerning him,[27]
   [As] cattle snorting against evil.

37 1 Also at this my heart trembles
     And leaps from its place.
   2 Pay attention to the raging of his voice
     And [the] rumbling that comes from his mouth.
   3 Beneath the whole heavens he flashes it,
     His lightning to the corners of the earth.
   4 After it a voice roars;
     He thunders with his majestic voice,
     And he does not delay them when his voice is heard.
   5 El thunders marvels with his voice;
     He does great things we cannot comprehend.

---

27. This is a difficult translation, but if correct it is different from the rebel in Job 26:14c, "Who can understand the thunder of his might."

6 For he commands to the snow, 'Fall to earth,'
   And [to the] shower, 'Rain,'
   And [there is] a shower of his mighty rains.
7 He seals up every human,
   As all mankind of his making knows.
8 [The] living [beast] has entered [its] lair,
   And in its den it lies down.
9 From the chamber comes the tempest
   And from [the] storehouses [the] cold.
10 From the breath of El comes ice,
   And [the] wide water is frozen.
11 Also with moisture he loads [the] clouds;
   He scatters his lightning [among the] clouds,
12 And it flashes about in every way with his guidance,
   Doing all that he commands,
   Upon the surface of the world [and] its earth.
13 Whether for discipline, or for his earth,
   Or for kindness, he makes it find [its mark].[28]
14 Give ear to this, O Job;
   Stand and consider the wonders of El.
15 Do you know how Eloah commands them,
   How he flashes lightning [from] his clouds? [29]
16 Do you know concerning [the] movements of clouds,
   The wonders of perfect knowledge?
17 You whose clothes are hot,
   When [the] earth is becalmed from [the] south,
18 Can you beat out the skies with him,
   Strong as a mirror of cast metal?
19 Tell us what we should say to him;
   We cannot arrange it in the presence of darkness.
20 Should it be told to him that I will speak?
   Does a man ask that he be swallowed up?

28. This God is to be feared, because he can strike you dead or help you. What a God!

29. Here Elihu is playing God. He questions the rebel Job even as Yahweh questioned the ancient Job from the whirlwind.

21 And now, they have not seen [the] light;
It was bright in the skies,
And the wind has passed; it cleared them.
22 From Zaphon[30] comes gold;
Over Eloah is awe-inspiring splendor.
23 We cannot find Shaddai,
Great [in] strength and justice,
And abundant righteousness, he will not oppress.
24 Therefore mankind should fear him;[31]
He does not pay attention to any who are wise of mind.[32]

---

30. This is the mountain where Baal built his temple. In Psalm 48:3 Mount Zion is called Zaphon.

31. So says the ancient Job and Job 28.

32. Therefore he pays attention to Elihu.

Afterword

Bringing together the many voices of Job in this book has been an enjoyable experience for me. It was essential initially to work on the individual voices one at a time, but when I began to bring them together, a real drama came into focus. I began to see it being acted out, and I became caught up in the narrative flow. I do not mean that *The Book of Job* is a drama, but the four main parts of Job functioned in my experience as a play in four acts that revealed the ongoing struggle of Israel's people to understand suffering and the nature of God. Since this struggle went on for many years, I realize that the time between each act of this play is varied, and today the play continues for us.

Before proceeding with the play, which evolved from my experience, it is important to remember the back-story. In ancient East Mediterranean Literature the old legend about one who suffers, who comes close to death, and then is rescued from the pit is ubiquitous. In these folk stories and priestly hymns, the sufferer repents, worships, and then is saved and blessed. In the ancient world people endured a great deal of suffering, but not without asking, "Why?" Others only sought to avoid suffering. Perhaps such stories gave them some hope. But a few knew that restoration was only an illusion. This fact is made clear in some Babylonian texts.

MISE EN SCÈNE

Act 1

Israel's literature was cosmopolitan. The Hebrew scribes taught the literature of their ancient Mediterranean neighbors to their students. And what about suffering? The people in ancient Israel suffered as much as anyone else in their world. In Israel's **Ancient Folktale of Job** the pattern is the same as in the earlier parallels. Job was a God-fearing man of integrity

Afterword

and he remained sinless. He suffered and he was tested. He did become angry at times, but after his interrogation by Yahweh, he repented. As in the other stories he was rescued and all was restored. It is a magnificent story, but is it true? In Israel a majority of the people and their leaders, including prophets, priests, scribes and kings, believed and lived by the ancient story of Job. It was great for both alter and state, because obedient God-fearing people are easy to handle. Yet, as this scene played out, the tension mounted.

Act 2

For centuries there was always a small minority who said, "We look around, and we see a different scene. The faithful suffer and die, and the sinners are in many instances doing just fine." So, there were those who rejected the traditional view of retribution. They did not believe in an all-powerful God, who demanded fear, rewarded the faithful, and punished the sinners. The minority did not know much about God, but they knew they needed to help each other. The scribe who wrote **The Rebel Job** belonged to the minority. As our drama enfolds, we cannot over estimate the power of the majority and the anger that propelled them to defeat a scribe who would attack the orthodox and produce a book whose aim was to crush **The Ancient Folktale of Job**. But the rebel Job believed the ancient story was built on illusion. Further, it was a cruel story and featured a cruel God. In fact, according to the rebel, the God of his opponents did not exist. The anger of the opponents rose to a point beyond control. But our rebel did not give in; he knew there was no justice and that we must help the powerless. That is all we can do, but it is enough.

Act 3

The rebel Job seems to have defeated his opponents in the debate contained in his poem, but the story continues. Later, an unknown author wrote the poem, "Where Can Wisdom Be Found?" This is a beautiful poem, and we can learn a lot about ancient mining and even something concerning an ancient understanding of geology from it. We also learn that mere humans cannot find wisdom. But the conclusion to the poem is

Afterword

disappointing. It reveals the voice of an editor who defends the position of the ancient Job: wisdom is yours if you will only fear God. The debate continues. In this scene the rebel is not defeated in any way, though here an editor ruined a great hymn, changing it in the final verse to support the point of view of the ancient Job.

Act 4

Later still, the anger of the majority, who were the fundamentalists of ancient Israel, caused them to re-group and present their arguments anew. Just as today fundamentalists might choose Pat Robertson, these ancient fundamentalist chose Elihu to do their bidding. In this scene, Elihu's speeches were supposed to finally defeat the rebel Job. He used old arguments against the rebel and produced a negative commentary against the rebel's poem. Elihu misquoted the rebel and in a pompous manner he played the role of God and interrogated the rebel. But as things have turned out, Elihu and his friends did win, because **The Rebel Job** is so surrounded by verbiage and hate that his gift to us has been lost. We must not create a final scene in this drama, but an enduring scene where the rebel Job finds his voice and speaks again.

Act 5

Actually we have been helped, because Archibald MacLeish has shown us how to create this scene in his play *J.B.* This world is great and interesting, but we will suffer in many ways; there will not be some kind of miraculous restoration. In *J.B.* the ending was not played that way. From the rebel we learn there is no justice, but love and compassion are possible. The fear of God has no place in this scene, and to see suffering as divine punishment is out of order. We need to listen to the voice of the rebel. The question is: how can we help the powerless? When the victims of Katrina cry out, who will respond? The God of the rebel's opponents does not and cannot hear. In this case, while individuals responded, the nation and state were also deaf. It is love that persuades us to respond, and for this insight I thank the rebel Job. This scene will continue to live and surrounds us with meaning.

Bibliography

Albright, W. F. "Some Canaanite-Phoenician Sources of Hebrew Wisdom." In *Wisdom in Israel and in the Ancient Near East*, edited by Martin Noth and D. Winton Thomas, 1–15. Supplements to Vetus Testamentum 3. Leiden: Brill, 1955.

Brooks, Geraldine. *Year of Wonders*. New York: Penguin, 2002.

Buber, Martin, and Franz Rosenzweig. *Die Fünf Bücher der Weisung*. Berlin: Schneider, 1930.

Cate, Curtis. *Friedrich Nietzsche*. New York: Overlook, 2005.

Cook, Stephen L. et al., editors. *The Whirlwind: Essays on Job, Hermeneutics and Theology in Memory of Jane Morse*. JSOTSup 336. London: Sheffield Academic, 2001.

Driver, Tom. "Third Thoughts on J.B." *Christian Century* (January 7, 1959) 106–7.

Eissfeldt, Otto. *The Old Testament: An Introduction*. Translated by P. R. Ackroyd. New York: Harper & Row, 1965.

Fisher, Loren. *Genesis: A Royal Epic*. Willits, CA: Fisher Publications, 2000.

———. *The Jerusalem Academy*. Willits, CA: Fisher Publications, 2002.

———. *Who Hears the Cries of the Innocent?* Willits, CA: Fisher Publications, 2002.

———. *The Minority Report: Silenced by Religion*. Willits, CA: Fisher Publications, 2004.

———. *The Rebel Job*. Willits, CA: Fisher Publications, 2006.

———. *The Rebel Job*. Rev. ed. Walnut Creek, CA: BookSurge, 2009.

———. *Tales from Ancient Egypt, The Birth of Stories*. Eugene, OR: Cascade Books, 2009.

Frigyesi, Judit. *Béla Bartók and Turn-of-the-Century Budapest*. Berkeley: University of California Press, 1998.

Funk, Robert W. *Jesus as Precursor*. Rev. ed. Edited by Edward Beutner. Sonoma, CA: Polebridge, 1994.

Funk, Robert W., Roy W. Hoover, and the Jesus Seminar. *The Five Gospels*. A Polebridge Press Book. New York: Macmillan, 1993.

Galston, David. "Postmodernism, the Historical Jesus, and the Church." *The Fourth R* (September–October 2005) 11–18.

Gass William. "A Forest of Bamboo." *Harper's* (August 2005) 83–89.

Gladwell, Malcolm. "The Cellular Church." *The New Yorker* (September 2005) 60–67.

Glatzer, Nahum N. *The Dimensions of Job: A Study and Selected Readings*. 1969. Reprinted, Eugene, OR: Wipf & Stock, 2002.

Good, Edwin M. *In Turns of Tempest*. Stanford: Stanford University Press, 1990.

Gordon, Cyrus H. *Ugaritic Literature*. Scripta Pontificii Instituti Biblici 98. Roma: Pontificium Institutum Biblicum. 1949.

———. "Belt Wrestling in the Ancient World." *HUCA* 23 (1950/51) 131–36.

———. "His Name is 'One.'" *JNES* 39 (1970) 198–99.

———. "Poetic Legends and Myths from Ugarit." *Berytus* 25 (1977) 5–131.

Gould, Stephen Jay. *Ever since Darwin*. New York: Norton, 1977.

Bibliography

Habel, Norman C. *The Book of Job: A Commentary*. Old Testament Library. Philadelphia: Westminster, 1985.

Hartshorne, Charles. *Omnipotence and Other Theological Mistakes*. Albany: State University of New York Press, 1984.

Havel, Václav. "Kosovo and the End of the Nation-State." *The New York Review of Books* (June 1999) 4–6.

Hone, Ralph E. *The Voice out of the Whirlwind: The Book of Job*. San Francisco: Chandler, 1960.

Johnson, A. R. "Mashal." In *Wisdom in Israel and the Ancient Near East*, edited by Martin Noth and D. Winton Thomas, 162–69. Supplements to Vetus Testamentum 3. Leiden: Brill, 1955.

Kertész, Imre. *Kaddish for a Child not Born*. Translated by Christopher C. Wilson and Katharina M. Wilson. Evanston: Northwestern University Press, 1997.

Kramer, Samuel Noah. "Man and His God: A Sumerian Variation on the 'Job' Motif." In *Wisdom in Israel and the Ancient Near East*, Edited by Martin Noth and D. Winton Thomas, 170–82. Supplements to Vetus Testamentum 3. Leiden: Brill, 1955.

Kraus, Clifford, Steven Lee Myers, Andrew C. Revkin, and Simon Romero. "As Polar Ice Turns to Water, Dreams of Treasure Abound." *The New York Times* (October 10, 2005).

Kushner, Harold S. *When Bad Things Happen to Good People*. 1981. Reprinted, New York: Avon, 1983.

Lambert, W. G. *Babylonian Wisdom Literature*. Oxford: Clarendon, 1967.

Leaves, Nigel. "The God Problem." *The Fourth R* (May/June 2005) 2–6, 20.

Lichtheim, Miriam. *Ancient Egyptian Literature*. Vol. 1. Berkeley: University of California Press, 1975.

Lustig, Arnošt. *Lovely Green Eyes*. Translated by Ewald Osers. New York: Arcade, 2002.

MacLeish, Archibald. *J.B.: A Play in Verse*. Boston: Houghton Mifflin, 1956.

Murphy, Roland E. "The Sage in Ecclesiastes and Qoheleth the Sage." In *The Sage in Israel and the Ancient Near East*, edited by John G. Gammie and Leo Perdue, 263–71. Winona Lake: Eisenbrauns, 1990.

Nietzsche, Friedrich. *The Gay Science*. Translated by Walter Kaufman. New York: Vintage, 1974.

Nougayrol, Jean. "Textes Suméro-Accadiens des Aarchives et Bibliothèques Privées díUgarit." In *Ugaritica V*, edited by Claude F. A. Schaeffer, 1–446. Mission de Ras Shamra 16. Paris: Imprimerie Nationale, 1968.

Pope, Marvin H. *Job*. 3rd ed. Anchor Bible 15. Garden City, NY: Doubleday, 1973.

Pritchard, James B., editor. *Ancient Near Eastern Texts Relating to the Old Testament*. 2nd ed. Princeton: Princeton University Press, 1955.

Roth, Joseph. *Hiob: Roman eines einfachen Mannes*. 1930. Reprinted, Amsterdam: de Lang, 1974.

———. *The Radetzky March*. Translated by Joachim Neugroschel. New York: Overlook, 2002.

———. *The Emperor's Tomb*. Translated by John Hoare. New York: Overlook, 2002.

———. *Job: The Story of a Simple Man*. Translated by Dorothy Thompson. New York: Overlook, 2003.

———. *What I Saw: Reports from Berlin, 1920–1933*. Translated by Michael Hofmann. New York: Norton, 2003.

Bibliography

Tanakh. The Holy Scriptures. Philadelphia: The Jewish Publication Society, 1985.
Terrien, Samuel. *Job: Poet of Existence.* Indianapolis: Bobbs-Merrill, 1957.
———. "*J.B.* and Job." *Christian Century* (January 7, 1959) 9–11.
———. *The Iconography of Job through the Centuries: Artists as Biblical Interpreters.* University Park: Pennsylvania State University Press, 1996.
Urquhart, Brian. "A Great Day in History." *The New York Review of Books* (January 15, 2004) 8–10.
Van Dusen, Henry P. Review of *J.B.* by Archibald MacLeish. *The Christian Century* (January 28, 1959) 106–7.
Virolleaud, Charles. *Le Palais Royal d'Ugarit, V: Textes alphabétiques des Archives Sud, Sud-ouest et du Petit-Palais.* Mission de Ras Shamra 11. Paris: Imprimerie Nationale, 1965.
Vollmann, William. "Friedrich Nietzsche: The Constructive Nihilist." *The New York Times* (August 14, 2005).
Whitehead, Alfred North. *Adventures of Ideas.* New York: Free Press, 1967.
Wiesel, Elie. *Night.* 1960. Reprinted, New York: Bantam, 1986.
———. *Night.* Translated by Marion Wiesel. New York: Hill & Wang, 2006.
Wolde, Ellen van. *Job 28: Cognition in Context.* Biblical Interpretation Series 64. Leiden: Brill, 2003.
———, editor. *Job's God.* Concilium 2004/4. London: SCM, 2004.
Wood, James. "Holiday in Hellmouth." *The New Yorker* (June 9–16, 2008) 86–92.
Zuckerman, Bruce. *Job The Silent.* Oxford: Oxford University Press, 1998.

Index of Ancient Deities and Characters of Myth and Legend

Adad, 54
Amon-Re, 54
Anat, 1, 15
Angels, 34
Anu, 54
Aqhat, 1
Baal, 1–2, 28, 31, 43, 54, 77, 98
Behemoth, 24
Danel, 1–3, 62
Dawn, 19
Dewy, 28
Dusk, 19
Earthy, 28
El, 1–2, 4, 8, 9, 24, 26, 35, 43, 53, 92
Eloah, 9, 30, 49, 50, 62, 73, 92
Elohim, 3, 6, 7, 8, 9, 14, 30, 32, 34, 35, 82, 91
Flashy, 28
Hayyin, 25–26
Holy Ones, 34
Keret, 1–2, 62

Koshar, 26
Leviathan, 24, 25, 26, 31
Lotan, 31
Marduk, 89
Mot, 10, 14, 19, 30, 47, 51, 62, 75, 88
Rahab, 44, 78
Resheph, 35
Satan, the, xvi, 3, 6, 7, 8, 73
Sekwi, 21
Shaddai/Shaddayan, 4, 8, 27, 36, 38, 65, 73
Shamesh, 42
Tannin, 40
Tehom, 19, 27, 81
Teman, 20, 43
Thoth, 21
Tiamat, 19, 81
Yahweh, xvi, xvii, 3, 5, 7, 8, 16, 18, 27, 28, 31, 34, 50, 54, 82, 85, 97, 100
Yamm, 19, 27, 31, 40, 43, 48, 81

Index of Ancient Documents

EGYPTIAN

A Dialogue between a Man and His Ba	3, 13, 29, 46
The Harper's Song	31, 40, 60, 64
The Story of Sinuhe	5, 42

AKKADIAN

The Babylonian Theodicy	xviii, 2, 33
I Will Praise the Lord of Wisdom	2, 89

UGARITIC

The Birth of the Gods (Dawn and Dusk)	19
Epic of Aqhat and Danel	1, 62
Epic of Keret	1, 2, 62
RS 25.460	xviii
UT 49:IV:29	54
UT 49:IV:40	54
UT 51:I:21	71
UT 68:27	19
UT 2059:21–23	14

HEBREW BIBLE

Genesis

	77
1–4	56
1:27	39
2	82
2:2	39
2:5–7	91
2:7	34
3:19b	46
4:23–24	35, 75
9:11	91
16:12	48
22	xvi, 73
30:3	31
33:19	28
38	82
50:23	31

Exodus

34:7	69

Numbers

24:7	4
24:15–19	4

Judges

	xii, xx

2 Samuel

12:15	82
14:11	65

Job

1–2	xi, xv, 3, 73
1:1b	3
1:6–12	xvi
1:7	5
1:9	7, 8
1:10–11	8
1:10	8
1:19	11
1:22	3
2	4
2:1–8	xvi
2:3	3
2:4	8
2:9–13	77
2:9	3
2:10	9
2:10b	3
2:11–13	xvii
3–26	xi, xii, xv, xvii, 2–3, 8, 17, 42, 77, 85, 87, 92
3	47
3:1	27
3:5	32, 47, 51
3:8	24
3:11	37
3:14	40
3:21	30
4:10–11	33
4:18	34
4:19	10, 46
4:20	60
5:1b	34
5:10	62
5:15	36
5:16	36
5:22	36
6:19	38
7:1	41
7:6a	39
7:7–21	40
7:8	41
7:9–10	40
7:10	60
7:11	46, 52
7:17	39
7:20	41
8:3	63
8:5–7	41
8:8	41
8:20	4
9	4, 51, 72
9:2–4	43
9:2	44
9:5–13	43
9:9	20
9:14–24	43
9:15	90
9:16	49
9:20–24	4
9:24	50, 63
9:31	14
9:31a	88
10	51
10:1	40, 52
10:9	10, 34
10:10–11	46
10:12	46
10:15	90
10:21	60
10:21b	51
10:22	49
11	49
11:6	52
12:2	49
12:3b	51
12:7–8	93
12:12	56
12:13	45, 63
12:18–21	13, 51
12:18a	51
12:21b	51
13	72
13:8b	52
13:15	xvi–xvii
13:15a	52

Index of Ancient Documents

Job (*continued*)

Reference	Page
13:20–27	53
14:1	16, 56
14:4	73
14:7–12	72
14:10	56, 57, 61, 66
15:15	34
15:15a	34
15:17–35	56
16:2–5	58
16:5	58
16:5b	58
16:6	58
16:6a	58
16:6	58
16:22	47, 60
17:8–10	60
17:11–16	61
17:13–14	14, 45, 88
17:15	66
18:7–10	61
19:7	45, 50, 63
19:23–24	ix
19:28	65
19:29	65
21:7	33
21:14a	71
21:16	68
21:16b	71
21:32–33	70
22:11b	20
22:18b	68
23	61, 93
23:3	72
23:5–7	72
23:8–9	72
23:9	66
23:13	16, 54
24:2–4	74
24:5–8	74
24:7	74
24:9	74
24:12	92
24:13–17	75
24:18–20	75
24:18	74
24:21–23a	75
24:23b–24	75
24:25	75
26	76
26:1–4	77
26:4	87
26:5–14	76
26:6	16
26:14a	24
26:14c	96
27–31	xi, xv
27	xvii, 3, 4, 77
27:1–23	3
27:1	10, 77
27:2	4, 90
27:4–5	4
27:5b–6a	4
27:8–23	4, 9, 75
27:8	9
28	xi, xii, xv, 98
28:7–8	80
28:28	83
29–31	3, 4
29	12
29:1—31:40	3
29:8	11
29:14	4
30	12
30:1	12
30:9	12
30:16	12
30:23	45, 88
30:23a	xix
31:3	17
31:6	4
31:9	17
31:15	54, 73
31:27	15
32–38	xii
32–37	xvi, 72, 85

32	xvii
32:1–5	85
32:1	85
32:3	85
32:5	85
33:4	86
33:18–30	14, 45, 88
33:18b	95
34:37	85
35:9–10	72
36:6–7	94
37:38–40	18
38–42	xi, xv, 3, 5
38:1	23
38:2	27
38:3	23
38:3a	51
38:3b	27
38:13	19
38:31–32	43
38:34	20
40:6–7	23
40:7b	27
40:10–13	23
40:25	24
41	25
41:13–17	26
41:18–21	26
42	xvii
42:7	30, 72
42:8	72

Psalms

8	39, 41
23:4	30
37:28	62
48	77
48:3	98
89:4	44
89:27–37	94

Proverbs

8:22	24
24:30–34	83
27:3	37

Ecclesiastes

4:5–6	84

Isaiah

	xii, xx
14:4–21	70
14:20	62
30:8	65
51:9	44

Jeremiah

16:5–9	64
20:14–18	30

Ezekiel

14:14	1, 3
14:20	1
28	1

Zechariah

14:9	16, 54

NEW TESTAMENT

Galatians

6:7–10	33

Index of Authors and Scholars

Albright, W. F., 5, 103
Brooks, Geraldine, 103
Buber, Martin, 35, 75, 103
Cate, Curtis, 103
Cobb, John B. Jr., 2
Cook, Stephen L., 103
Driver, Tom, xi, 103
Eissfeldt, Otto, 4, 103
Fisher, Loren R., xviii, 2, 29, 30, 46, 64, 103
Frigyesi, Judit, 103
Funk, Robert W., 103
Galston, David, 103
Gass, William
Ginsberg, H. L., xvii, 3, 37, 51
Gladwell, Malcolm, 103
Glatzer, Nahum N., xv, 103
Good, Edwin M., ix, xvi, xix, xx, 39, 60, 90, 103
Gordon, Cyrus H., 2, 16, 19, 51, 54, 62, 103
Gould, Stephen J., 103
Habel, Norman C., 53, 104
Hartshorne, Charles, 104
Havel, Václav, 104
Hone, Ralph E., xi–xii, 104
Hoover, Roy W., 103
Johnson, A. R., 3, 104
Kertéz, Imre, 104
Kramer, Samuel Noah, xviii, 2, 104
Kraus, Clifford, 104
Kushner, Harold S., 104
Lambert, W. G., xviii, 2, 33, 42, 89, 104
Leaves, Nigel, 104

Lichtheim, Miriam, 31, 40, 60, 64, 104
Lustig, Anošt, 104
MacLeish, Archibald, ix–xii, 101, 104
Murphy, Roland E., 104
Myers, Stephen Lee, 104
Nietzsche, Friedrich, 104
Nougayrol, Jean, xviii, 104
Pixley, Jorge V., 3
Pope, Marvin H., ix, xv, xvii, xviii, xx, 3, 4, 5, 6, 9, 10, 19, 20, 21, 22, 23, 24, 25, 32, 35, 39, 43, 47, 48, 49, 51, 52, 58, 62, 65, 67, 75, 76, 77, 88, 90, 104
Pritchard, James B., 104
Revkin, Andrew C., 104
Romero, Simon, 104
Rosenzweig, Franz, 35, 75, 103
Roth, Joseph, ix, 104
Sanders, James A., 3
Schaeffer, Claude F. A., 104
Terrien, Samuel, xi, 105
Tur-Sinai, N. H., xi
Urquhart, Brian, 105
Van Dusen, Henry P., xi–xii, 105
Virolleaud, Charles, 105
Vollmann, William, 105
Whitehead, Alfred North, 105
Wiesel, Elie, 105
Wilcox, John T., 3
Wolde, Ellen van, 105
Wood, James, 105
Zevit, Ziony, 2
Zuckerman, Bruce, ix, 105

www.ingramcontent.com/pod-product-compliance
Lightning Source LLC
Chambersburg PA
CBHW030902170426
43193CB00009BA/710